THE · SCIENCE · OF
HURDLING
BY · BRENT · MCFARLANE

Canadian Track and Field
Association
Canadienne d'Athlétisme

Canadian Cataloguing in Publication Data

McFarlane, A. Brent, 1948-
The Science of Hurdling

Bibliography: p.
ISBN 0-919375-48-0

1. Hurdle-racing. I. Canadian Track and
Field Association. II. Title.

GV1067.M34 1988   796.4'26   C88-090058-X

Editor	Roger Burrows
Photography	Claus Anderson
	Jim Merrithew (cover)
Typesetting	The Runge Press Limited, Ottawa
Cover Design	Michael Donnelly
Illustrations	Bill Arnold and Michael Donnelly
Printing	Dollco Printing, Ottawa
Published 1988	The Canadian Track and Field Association
	333 River Road, Ottawa, Ontario
	Canada K1L 8H9

To my wife Vicki, son Christopher and daughter Andrea.

THANKS for your understanding.

EDITOR'S INTRODUCTION

Brent McFarlane is familiar to many devotees of hurdling from his many previous publications and his appearance at clinics, workshops and symposia all over the world. His second book "Understanding the Hurdle Events" has been used as a standard text for Canadian hurdling coaches ever since its publication in 1981.

This third book is an extension and development of the previous one. Readers who know his work will recognize many of his cherished precepts: the identification of components of training, the need to sequence training for best effect and above all, the concept of rhythm.

Every event has its rhythm. A shotputter feels it when every element of a single throw falls into place at precisely the right time. A marathoner feels it when, despite the pressing fatigue, there is a glorious sensation of control.

But perhaps it is in the hurdles where the rhythm can best be shared with the widest audience. In the hands of an accomplished athlete, the event is patently a thing of beauty. The hurdles stand like bar lines on a musical score, not "in the way", but simply circumscribing the precision, power and grace to be displayed during the run. The great hurdlers, the Moses', Erhardt's and Nehemiah's, do not jump the hurdles, they flow over them like a great musician flows through the strict tempi of Bach.

Brent McFarlane feels the beauty, but he also knows that each inspired – or less than inspired – performance is the product of hours, months and years of careful and difficult practice. This is why the book is called "The Science of Hurdling". True, it is not loaded down with experimental data and pure research, although those interested will find an extensive bibliography for their further study. This is "science" almost in the classical sense of "knowledge". Brent explains what makes up a hurdler and a successful hurdling career and what is needed for the athlete to develop to full potential. He hopes that athletes and coaches will not be disappointed to learn what performers in other fields have known for centuries: it takes hard work, correctly done and constantly rehearsed.

The Canadian Track and Field Association is proud to have worked with Brent in the production of this book.

His commitment to the event and to the education of other coaches has been evident from the outset. He is an expert: his programme constantly develops top Canadian hurdlers in less than ideal conditions. But he is above all an extremely effective educator. Students in his elementary school know this every time he enters a classroom. The CTFA is delighted to spread the news a little wider.

Roger Burrows

ABOUT THE AUTHOR

Brent McFarlane is an honours graduate in Kinesiology and Science from the University of Waterloo and now works as a teacher.

As an athlete, he competed in sprints and middle distance events. It is as coach and educator that he has made his mark on the sport in Canada and elsewhere. For over a decade he has studied and written extensively, primarily on the hurdle events. He has conducted countless clinics and workshops in various aspects of the events and has been the major contributor to the design of the CTFA's hurdling education programme.

He is presently the Hurdles Representative on the CTFA's National Programme Committee and continues to coach National Team delegations at major competitions (including three Olympic Games, two Commonwealth Games and two World Championships) as he has done since his first assignment in 1975.

With all his national and international involvement, he still coaches on a daily basis with the Kitchener-Waterloo T.C., his club of many years.

He lives in Waterloo, Ontario with his wife Vicki and two children Chris and Andrea.

ACKNOWLEDGMENT AND THANKS

In trying to present one interpretation about the hurdle events, I wish to acknowledge and thank several world authorities and friends for giving me the opportunity to become an educator and coach. With respect and gratitude, I wish to state my deep indebtedness to:

Alexander Ewen (Scotland), Svenn Folkman (Denmark), Esko Olkonen (Finland), Tadeusz Szczepanski (Poland), Alessandro and Gabre Calvesi (Italy), Emil Dostal (Czech), Gerard Mach (Canada), Hannelore Keydel (West Germany), Dr. Herve Stephan (France), Mike Houston (Canada), Frank Dick (England), Charlie Francis (Canada), Mike McClemont (Canada), Cecil Smith (Canada), Bogdan Poprawski (Canada), Kenth Olsson (Sweden), Denis Landry (Canada), Craig Poole (USA), Pat Reid (Canada), John Powell (Canada), Tudor Bompa (Canada), Luc Bienvenue (Canada).

SPECIAL THANKS

To Roger Burrows (CTFA) for the enormous amount of time and patience he showed in putting the final draft of this book together. Without him none of this would have appeared!

SPECIAL ACKNOWLEDGMENT TO
ADIDAS CANADA

To adidas Canada for the support they have provided to me and to my athletes throughout my coaching career. Their contribution has been a special and selfless one.

AUTHOR'S INTRODUCTION

It is my intention that the contents of this hurdling book represent a reservoir of coaching experience, knowledge and the application of information from around the world.

There are two purposes for this book. Firstly, to study the 'science' of hurdling, that is the biomechanics, physiology and psychology necessary to be successful in each of the hurdle events. This expansion of one's knowledge, by studying more detailed materials, texts and articles gives a coach the ability to come as 'close to the truth' about training and its effects as can be expected for a given environment.

Secondly, this book will coincide with the National Coaching Certification Program. It was written for those who already have achieved Level 2 (theory, technical and practical) from the Coaching Association of Canada and the Canadian Track and Field Association and who are ready to proceed to Level 3. With it, the Level 3 coach will be able to apply current information at a national and international level.

The "art" of coaching lies with each individual coach. The qualities of a good coach differ from person to person. All have their own uniqueness. Hopefully, this book will bridge the gap for those who read it and apply the science to art!

Brent McFarlane

TABLE OF CONTENTS

LIST OF TABLES, DIAGRAMS AND FIGURES

Cover Photo: Mark McKoy, Canada's top hurdler.

CHAPTER 1

THE HURDLE EVENTS

*"There shall be ten flights of hurdles
in each lane..."*

CHAPTER AT A GLANCE

INTRODUCTION

110m HURDLES
Introduction
The Start and Sprint Approach to First Hurdle
Hurdle Clearance
   (1) Lead Leg
   (2) Trail Leg
   (3) Arm Action
   (4) Body Lean
Landing and Follow Up Stride
Running Between Hurdles
Finishing Sprint

100m HURDLES

400m HURDLES
Start & Sprint Approach To First Hurdle
Hurdle Clearance
Stride Pattern & Running Between Hurdles
Run in

INTRODUCTION

The International Amateur Athletic Federation (IAAF) rules governing hurdling are found in the Federation's handbook (Rule 163) and are set out in Table 1-1. The prescribed specifications for each hurdle race are listed in Table 1-2. It is also important to realize that variations of these specifications may be in effect for age class competition held under different jurisdictions.

Many of the basic rules and principles of biomechanics are listed in Table 1-3. Differences in the interpretation of the "correct" biomechanics of hurdling have led to a variety of successful styles. However, a knowledge of the biomechanics of human motion is a major concern if a coach is to use the most efficient mechanical principles to maximize an athlete's hurdling performance.

The 110m high hurdles for men is technically the most difficult of the hurdle events and therefore will be dealt with first in full detail. The other 3 hurdle events (100m hurdles for women, 400m hurdles for men and women) will then be examined for the point of view in which they are different from the 110m hurdles or otherwise unique.

Table 1-1 IAAF Rules Governing Hurdling

Rule 163 Hurdle Races

1. Distances. The following are the standard distances:

MEN	WOMEN
110,400 metres	100,400 metres

There shall be ten flights of hurdles in each lane... . The hurdle shall be so placed on the track that the feet of the hurdle shall be on the side of the approach by the competitor.

2. Construction. The hurdles shall be made of metal or some other suitable material with the top bar of wood or other suitable material. They shall consist of two bases and two uprights supporting a rectangular frame, reinforced by one or more cross-bars, the uprights to be fixed at the extreme end of each base. The hurdle shall be of such a design that a force at least equal to the

3

weight of 3.6 kilograms applied to the centre of the top edge of the top bar is required to overturn it. The hurdle may be adjustable in height for each event. The counterweights must be adjustable so that at each height a force at least equal to the weight of 3.6 kilograms and not more than 4 kilograms is required to overturn it.

NOTE – To check the resisting force of hurdles a simple spring balance should be used by the application of pulling force to the centre of the top bar. Alternatively use a cord with a hook, applied to the centre of the top bar, take the cord along over a pulley fixed conveniently and load the other end of the cord with weights.

Table 1-2 Hurdle Specifications

Hurdle Specifications

Distance	No. of Hurdles	Distance to 1st Hurdle	Distance Between	Height	Notes
MALE					
80m	8	12m	8m	84cm (2'9")*	(a)
100m	10	12m	8.50m	91.5cm (3'0")*	(a)
110m	10	13.72m	9.14m	106.7cm (3'6")*	(a)
200m	10	18.29m	18.29m	76cm (2'6")	now seldom held
300m	7	50m	35m	91.5cm (3'0")*	
400m	10	45m	35m	91.5cm (3'0")	
FEMALE					
80m	8	12m	8m	76cm (2'6")*	(a)
100m	10	13m	8.50m	84cm (2'9")	(a)
200m	10	16m	19m	76cm (2'6")	now seldom held
300m	7	50m	35m	76cm (2'6")*	
400m	10	45m	35m	76cm (2'6")	

NOTES

(a) These specifications are also used for equivalent *indoor* events. Usual distances are 50m (4 hurdles) or 60m (5 hurdles).

* These specifications are used for age class or school competition. There are often variations, especially for the younger age classes. It is advisable to check with the appropriate governing body for exact details.

COMMENTS

1: Competitors in the nationally and internationally recognized Junior categories use the same specifications as Seniors.

2: Specifications for the category immediately below Junior vary between jurisdictions. They represent attempts to compromise between the younger age class specifications and those used for Junior/Senior. The *recommended progression* is to increase the height of the hurdles while not increasing the distance between. This teaches good clearance technique while maintaining quick rhythm. In the short events, the recommendations are:

> **Boys** – 100m hurdles at 99cm (3'3"),
> **Girls** – 80m hurdles at 84cm (2'9").

Table 1-3 Basic Rules & Principles of Biomechanics

Simplified Biomechanics
A glossary, courtesy of Fred Wilt

1. Mechanics is a branch of physics which deals with the inter-relations of force.
2. Motion is a continuous change of position.
3. Moment of inertia is mass times radius squared.
4. Newton's first law (the Law of Inertia) shows that a body at rest or in uniform straight line motion will continue in that state until compelled to change by an external force.
5. Newton's second law (the Law of Acceleration) shows that acceleration is proportional to force and inversely proportional to mass.
6. Newton's third law of motion (the Law of Reaction) states that to every action there is an equal and opposite reaction.
7. Force is mass times acceleration.
8. Linear motion is straight line movement from one point to another.
9. Velocity is rate of change of position in a given direction. Momentum is mass times velocity.
11. Angular velocity is the angle through which a body turns per second.
12. Static produces a force without producing motion.
13. Acceleration is the rate of change of velocity.
14. Impulse is force multiplied by time.
15. Inertia is the body's resistance to change of motion.

16. An axis is a straight line about which a body rotates.
17. Angular acceleration is the rate of change of angular velocity.
18. The centre of gravity is the point in a body where force acts.
19. Centrifugal force is the force pulling outward during rotation.
20. Eccentric thrust is an off-centre thrust.
21. Energy is the capacity to do work.
22. Gravity is the force which causes objects to move vertically downward towards the centre of the earth.
23. The acceleration of a free falling object is 9.8m/second or 32ft/second.
24. Negative acceleration means deceleration or decreasing the velocity.
25. Speed = stride length × stride frequency.
26. Uniform motion is steady, constant motion with unchanging speed.
27. Torque is the force causing an object to rotate, or force × length of lever arm.
28. Speed is the rate of change of position.
29. Power means rate of work, or work divided by time.
30. Positive acceleration means increasing the velocity faster and faster.
31. Work is force times distance in the direction of force.
32. Centripetal force is the force pulling inward during rotation.
33. The application of Newton's first law to *angular* motion shows that a body does not change its angular velocity unless acted upon by an external, unbalanced torque.
34. Balance or equilibrium exists when the resultant of all forces acting on a body are zero.
35. Mechanical work = product of weight lifted × distance lifted.
36. The sagittal axis of the body is an axis parallel to the ground which passes through the body from front to back or anteroposterior axis.
37. The frontal axis of the body is an axis parallel to the ground passing through the body from side to side.
38. The horizontal or transverse axis is an axis which is parallel to the ground.
39. Angular momentum is moment of inertia × angular velocity.
40. The most common body lever is the "third class lever" where the force is situated between the fulcrum and the resistance.

THE 110m HURDLES

The men's 110m hurdles is fundamentally a faultless sprint over 10 equally spaced, 106.7cm (42") barriers. **Sprint** and **faultless** are the key words. Speed, the number one pre-requisite for a hurdler, is the product of stride length and stride frequency.

Most hurdlers take 8 strides to the first hurdle and 3 strides between hurdles. As a result, the stride length and number of strides are controlled. Stride frequency is therefore the determining factor of speed in the event. Ideally, a potential hurdler should possess 10.5 second or better 100m speed. Add faultless technique to this speed and you have a hurdler with potential.

For convenience this sprint hurdle event will be divided into five basic phases:

(1) start and sprint approach to the first hurdle,
(2) hurdle clearance,
(3) landing,
(4) running between hurdles,
(5) finishing sprint.

Take-off

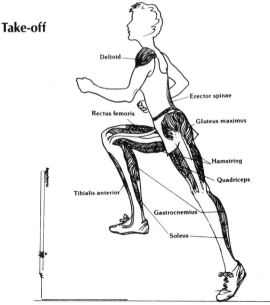

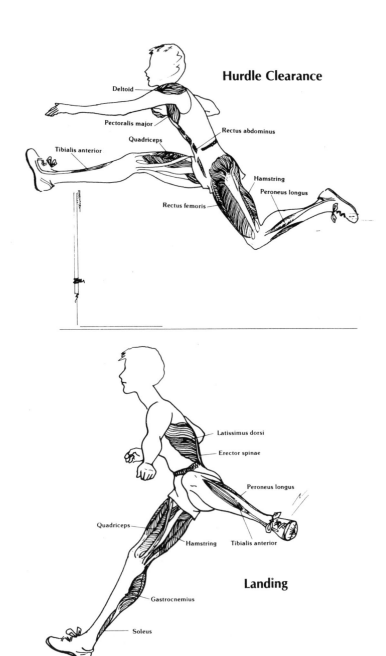

Hurdle Clearance

Deltoid

Pectoralis major

Rectus abdominus

Quadriceps

Tibialis anterior

Hamstring

Peroneus longus

Rectus femoris

Latissimus dorsi

Erector spinae

Peroneus longus

Quadriceps

Hamstring

Tibialis anterior

Gastrocnemius

Landing

Soleus

Muscle groups involved in the hurdling action. *(Courtesy National Strength and Conditioning Journal)* – *January 1987.*

The Start and Sprint Approach to the First Hurdle

To cover the 13.72m to the first hurdle with the normal 8 stride approach requires the trail leg to be on the front starting block. A good medium start position has the front foot approximately 45cm behind the start line and the knee of the rear leg opposite the toe of the front foot.

At the gun, the back foot is pulled from the blocks. Simultaneously, the arms begin the acceleration of properly balanced and forward strides. The stride length progressively lengthens until the next-to-last stride before take-off. The last stride before take-off is shorter than the previous one. A sprinter reaches his normal running action after 20 to 25m while hurdlers must reach this point after 4 or 5 strides from the blocks.

It must be appreciated that each phase of this event is dependent on attaining maximum speed in the initial 13.72m and over the first 2 hurdles. **Hurdling is sprinting.** The pattern is not 3 strides and a jump, but a continuous 4 stride pattern with the last stride merely longer and more accentuated in its action because of the presence of the barrier. Any change in speed depends on the impulse (force × time) of the foot on the ground from force applied at the hip, knee and ankle joints.

A few tall, elite athletes are able to use 7 strides to the first hurdle with the trail leg in the back block. However, acceleration can only be obtained by stride frequency, not stride length. A 7-stride approach does not facilitate this acceleration. The possible problems of over-striding, the accompanying "braking" effect on foot placement, and other complications which result from the change in rhythm (from the slower pattern of 7 strides to the quicker 3 stride pattern between hurdles), are considered a disadvantage.

Hurdle Clearance

The athlete's distance from the hurdle on take-off will depend on several factors: speed of the approach run, length and speed of the lead leg, height of the athlete and the hurdle, flexibility of the hip and knee joints, type of track surface, weather conditions, previous hurdle clearance, and the athlete's kinesthetic "feel" for the hurdle.

The take-off is 2.00–2.20m from the hurdle while the landing is 1.15–1.30m from the hurdle. Take-off is therefore about 60% of the total flight with the landing about 40%. The take-off varies throughout the race. As speed increases over the initial hurdles, likewise does the take-off distance, with the landing distance decreasing. Towards the end of the race the take-off and landing distances approach that of the initial phases since some fatigue has set in and loss of speed occurs. (See Table 1-4)

Four actions deserve attention in this phase of hurdling:

(1) lead leg,
(2) trail leg,
(3) arm action,
(4) body lean.

(1) Lead leg: This action begins with a vigorous, quick high knee lift, straight up and down in the line of running. This flexed knee must reach its high point (beyond the horizontal to the chest with the heel under the body) before the lower leg swings forward. This action decreases the moment of inertia about the hip while increasing the lead leg's angular velocity. This high knee action brings with it a complete and brief extension of the knee joint of the trail leg in a position known as "stretched tall". The lead foot should not be allowed to "escape" or get in front of the attacking knee. This common error causes a drop in the centre of gravity, lower hips, and problems with the knee locking, which will delay the clearance.

Table 1-4 Hurdle Clearance

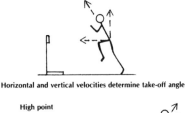

Horizontal and vertical velocities determine take-off angle

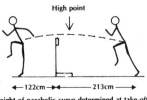

High point

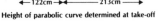

←—122cm—→←————213cm————→

Height of parabolic curve determined at take-off

Action and Reaction
(leg and trunk)

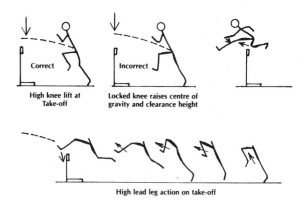

High knee lift at Take-off

Locked knee raises centre of gravity and clearance height

High lead leg action on take-off

The lower lead leg is now thrust toward the hurdle like a karate kick and then immediately pulled actively downward and under the body in the sagittal plane. The landing of the lead leg must be very dynamic and decisive. Valuable time can be gained by actively pulling the leg quickly down behind the hurdle rail to get the best possible landing position. This assists the fast follow-up step of the trail leg. Good hurdlers avoid the braking action associated with the landing by keeping the centre of gravity in front of the support leg and staying tall so the heel does not collapse to the ground.

Controversy surrounds the question of whether the lead leg crosses the hurdle flexed or straight. It appears that the lead leg does become flexed momentarily before crossing the hurdle. The high point of the heel of the lead leg occurs approximately 30cm from the hurdle rail. At this point the leg begins to flex to cross the hurdle. By contrast, a locked knee on the hurdle indicates poor lead leg action and poor flexibility in the hip. The result is that the athlete jumps over the hurdle and loses speed.

The lead leg must be allowed to attack the hurdle in a straight horizontal line. If a hurdler is too close to the hurdle, he will jump it; if too far away, he may hit it. Taller hurdlers (1.85m +) can afford to get closer to the hurdle since they do not have to raise their centre of gravity as high in clearance as the shorter hurdlers.

(2) Trail leg: The main purpose of the trail leg is to perform a fast follow-up stride with no errors. The trail leg action does not begin until the lead foot is near the hurdle rail. This underlines the importance of a mechanically sound lead leg action. The degree of extension of the knee of the trail leg indicates the extent to which the action was hurried or fully completed. The trail leg is then advanced forward as the toe becomes everted and the thigh moves to a position parallel to the hurdle rail. This action (a hip circle) is at right angles to the body. The heel of the trail leg must remain close to the seat until it crosses the hurdle, at which time it is pulled by the high knee to the under-the-arm position.

The trail leg must then move from the hurdle in a running action. If the take-off occurs too soon, the trail leg will be pulled through prematurely and a braking effect will result because the lead leg will not have landed. No interruption should occur upon landing if the continuous hurdling action is to be maintained.

(3) Arm action: As the lead leg is lifted and extended towards the hurdle, the lead (or opposite) arm is brought forward slighty flexed in front of the chest and then allowed to extend of its own accord. It should not be thrust forward violently as this exaggerates and twists the upper body. Synchronization of arm action with leg action helps to keep the shoulders square, assists balance and timing, and counteracts the lateral rotations of the trunk. It is for these reasons that the use of a single arm or a one-and-a-half arm take-off is recommended. Using a double arm action puts the arms out of the running phase and places the hurdler in an uncoordinated position when landing. The arm action should be as close to one's sprinting action as possible. The trail arm simply moves in a short circle near the hip, allowing it to enter the sprinting phase upon landing.

As the trail leg comes forward, the equal and opposite reaction is the backward motion or "pawing" of the lead arm. If these two actions are not equal and opposite, the shoulders will not remain square throughout flight and landing. Since the leg has more mass than the arm, the arm must swing wider than the leg to counteract its actions. The pawing action is terminated as soon as the lead leg hits the ground.

(4) Body Lean: For an effective "stretched tall" position (which ultimately affects the take-off), body lean and forward rotation must start while the hurdler is in contact with the ground. The path of the centre of gravity takes a parabolic curve, which cannot be altered once in flight other than by external forces. To aid this, a shortened stride is taken prior to the take-off. The lean helps to keep the centre of gravity as close to its normal sprinting path as the hurdle height will permit. Strength in the abdominal muscles permits an easy and effective forward lean, while strength in the back provides a quick recovery from the lean to a more upright running position once the hurdle is cleared.

Landing and Follow-up Stride

Upon landing the trail leg knee must be pulled through high. Although the follow-up stride is shorter, it will be too short if this knee is allowed to drop. The centre of gravity should be slightly ahead of the body with a good active ball to toe rolling action. A lead leg landing (touch-down) between 1.15 to 1.30m and a follow-up stride between 1.52 and 1.62m is necessary to maintain running frequency for the remaining 2 strides. Attention is now on sprinting, running tall and an active foot placement.

Running Between Hurdles

Analysis of the set and precise 3 stride pattern over the 9.14m distance between hurdles now indicates the importance of rhythm coupled with speed. The consistency of a 1.0 to 1.1 second touchdown time (time from lead leg landing between 2 consecutive hurdles) of top hurdlers allows no margin for mechanical errors and little time for adjustments in balance, timing or stride pattern. Any mechanical errors during clearance can result in the common problems of "braking" upon landing, running flat-footed, low hips and centre of gravity, overstriding and most obvious, the loss of speed.

The 3 strides between hurdles are shorter than normal. The follow-up stride is always the shortest (1.52 to 1.62m) since its driving force is reduced by the preceding hurdle clearance. The second stride must be the longest (2.00 to

2.20m). The third and last stride is always slightly shorter than the previous stride as it prepares the body for the hurdle attack (lean) and assists the trajectory of the centre of gravity on its parabolic curve during clearance. No loss of speed can occur during clearance or between hurdles from mechanical or energy losses which result from careless errors. It must always be remembered that hurdling is a unified and faultless sprint, rhythmically run over 10 barriers.

The 110m hurdle race is really made up of three parts:
(1) the acceleration phase to maximum speed which ends around the third hurdle
(2) the maintenance of maximum speed until the eighth hurdle
(3) deceleration over the last two hurdles because of the onset of fatigue.

Finishing Sprint

Having cleared the last hurdle all attention is directed immediately towards the remaining 14.20m to the finish line. Athletes should count their strides and dip on the last stride.

THE 100 METRE HURDLES

The sprint hurdle event for women has not always been 100m in length. The 80m hurdle race was introduced into the Olympic Games in 1932, with a winning time of 11.7 seconds. The world record (now discontinued) of 10.3 is held by Maureen Caird of Australia, set in the 1968 Olympic Games.

The rapid development of the strength and speed of women athletes meant a revision of the specifications to allow higher barriers with more distance between. In 1969, a new event, the 100m hurdles was introduced — 10 hurdles, 13m to the first hurdle, each 84cm (33″) in height and 8.5m between hurdles. Such is the advance in the sport that the 80m hurdles is now the usual event for girls in age class competition.

Much of what was said in the 110m hurdles applies to the 100m hurdles. There are, however, two basic differences.

Firstly, the clearance stride over the hurdle is shorter for women, 2.84 to 2.94m as compared with a 3.15–3.50m clearance for the men. The take-off distance will vary from 1.95 to 2.10m and the landing .80 to 1.00m. The female hurdler touches down closer to the hurdle than her male counterpart. The take-off stride is shortened, similar to that of the 110m hurdler. This shortened stride allows the aggressive lead leg to attack the hurdle more quickly. Secondly, the lower height of the hurdle allows the trail leg of the female to be brought through in a less pronounced manner than the high "under the arm" position of the men's hurdles. The trail leg should be pulled through quickly, emphasizing pulling the heel forward from the seat for an active landing.

Speed and rhythm are as indispensible as in the men's event. The difference between the flat 100m and the 100m hurdles should range from 1.5 to 2.0 seconds.

Only by rehearsing all parts of this race can the kinesthetic feel of sprint hurdling be learned and programmed into the body.

Table 1-5 Rhythm Chart
(Leading Women Hurdlers of past Olympics)

	H1	H2	H3	H4	H5	H6	H7	H8	H9	H10	Finish Time
Ehrhardt											
1972		3.6	4.6	5.6	6.5	7.5	8.5	9.5	10.4	11.5	
DDR	2.5	(1.1)	(1.0)	(1.0)	(1.0)	(1.0)	(1.0)	(1.0)	(0.9)	(1.1)	12.59
Schaller											
1976		3.6	4.6	5.6	6.5	7.5	8.5	9.5	10.5	11.6	
DDR	2.5	(1.1)	(1.0)	(1.0)	(1.0)	(1.0)	(1.0)	(1.0)	(1.0)	(1.1)	12.77
Anisimova											
1976		3.6	4.6	5.6	6.6	7.6	8.6	9.6	10.6	11.6	
USSR	2.5	(1.1)	(1.0)	(1.0)	(1.0)	(1.0)	(1.0)	(1.0)	(1.0)	(1.0)	12.78
Komisova											
1980		3.5	4.5	5.5	6.5	7.5	8.5	9.5	10.5	11.5	
USSR	2.5	(1.0)	(1.0)	(1.0)	(1.0)	(1.0)	(1.0)	(1.0)	(1.0)		12.56

The figures in Table 1-5 (taken from Olympic competition) show that **rhythm** plays a major role. The 1.0 seconds between hurdles (or better by Erhardt) indicates the rehearsal of all parts of this race to be totally complete. There is no margin for error. The Eastern Europeans particularly, have shown us that no detail of preparation can

1

2

3

4

The final of the 100m hurdles in the 1986 Commonwealth Games. Canada's Julie Rocheleau (4th – 13.46) battles eventual silver medalist Wendy Teal (ENG – 13.41). Students of hurdling will note small, but critical breakdowns in technique under the strain of tough competition. (But nothing like the breakdown in technique which occurs in the lane to Rocheleau's right!).

be neglected or left to chance.

Although second to rhythm, speed is close. Coaches should not give their athletes the impression that "if you cannot sprint become a hurdler". A hurdler without good sprinting speed will have limited success.

THE 400M HURDLES

The 400m hurdles for both men and women is a specialist event requiring expertise and experience. It is the most strenuous of all the hurdle events. There are 10 hurdles placed 35m apart with a 45m run to the first hurdle, a 40m run-in and hurdle heights of 91.5cm (36") for men and 76.0cm (30") for women. The immense area for error must be minimized by rehearsing and adopting a race plan that suits all possible situations.

The qualities necessary for 400m hurdling specialists are:

(1) Special Endurance 1 and 2 (See Chapter 3): the ability to run a fast 400m flat
(2) Skill: competent hurdling with either lead leg
(3) Race plan: adopting a definite race plan with a proper stride pattern, pace judgement and 200m differentials
(4) Special awareness: modifying the race plan due to the weather, track surface, lane assignment, poor hurdle clearance.

The 400m hurdles, which still must be considered a sprint hurdle event, will be examined in four parts.

(1) start and sprint approach to the first hurdle
(2) hurdle clearance
(3) stride pattern and running between hurdles
(4) the run-in.

The Start and Sprint Approach to the First Hurdle

In covering the 45m to the first hurdle, most male hurdlers use 22 strides, which places the trail leg in the front block. For 21, 23 or 25 strides the trail leg is in the back block. It is useful to count the number of strides to the first hurdle as follows: for 21, 23 and 25 strides, the trail leg will contact the track 11, 12 and 13 times and for 22 and 24 it will make contact 11 and 12 times respectively. The acceleration phase from the blocks for the first 8–10 strides is similar to that of the 400m runner. The last 4–5 strides before the hurdle are more controlled as they set the rhythm for the clearance.

Hurdle Clearance

The basic mechanics of hurdling continue to apply. The lower hurdle heights (91.5cm men; 76.0cm women) and slower forward speed allow for a slower pivot and less body lean over the hurdle. On the other hand, fatigue magnifies errors in technique. For this reason emphasis must be placed on conditioning, rehearsal and planning for all possible race conditions.

From the technical point of view the 400m hurdles does not receive enough attention. The hips must stay tall and move forward throughout the clearance to maintain the running rhythm. If they fall, loss of horizontal speed and an increased number of strides between hurdles will result. Since horizontal speed is less than in sprint hurdles, it seems that less emphasis is placed on the aggressive attack of the lead leg, running rhythm and hip flexibility. Neglect here is a mistake!

Stride Pattern and Running Between Hurdles

The difference between a flat 400m and 400m hurdle race can vary between 3 seconds at world class level to 5 seconds at age class level. Women have only just started to specialize in the event. They have the advantage of learning from the many years of experience and mistakes of the men to bring down this differential.

Hurdlers with greater leg length (and consequently stride length), have a distinct advantage in 400m hurdling. Firstly, a naturally longer stride reduces the number of total strides taken in a race. Secondly, the number of strides to the first hurdle and between hurdles is dictated by the athlete's natural stride length. Table 1-6 shows the length of stride required for a given number of strides between hurdles.

Table 1-6 Stride Length and Stride Number

Strides Between Hurdles	Required Stride Length
12	2.68m (8'9")
13	2.45m (8'0")
14	2.27m (7'6")
15	2.13m (7'0")
16	2.00m (6'6")
17	1.85m (6'1")
18	1.64m (5'5")

The immense differentiation offered in stride pattern must be minimized. Most hurdlers use 13, 15 or 17 strides between hurdles with a possible change-down to 14 or 16 at hurdles 5 to 7. This means alternating lead legs and a modified rhythm change. Chopping or overstriding between hurdles indicates problems in stride pattern which the athlete has not worked to correct. The athlete must once again count the trail leg contacts (every other stride) during the entire race. For 13, 15 and 17 strides the trail leg will contact 7, 8 and 9 times respectively.

The data in Table 1-7 makes it clear that stride length plays a major role in the overall racing plan and results. In Akii-Bua's Olympic victory in 1972, he took 162 strides to defeat Hemery at 164 and Mann at 166 strides. Had these two men been able to alternate lead legs after hurdle 5, their total strides would have been 161 and 163 respectively giving rise to intriguing speculation about the final outcome! Edwin Moses (1976 and 1984 Olympic Champion and World Champion in 1983) running at 153 strides (excluding clearance strides) is considering 12 strides for the first 3 hurdles indicating the possiblility of a 46.? 400m hurdles run.

Table 1-7 Stride Analysis – 400m Hurdles

Hurdle	Akii-Bua (Uganda) (Munich) 1972 TD	Moses (USA) (Montreal) 1976 TD	Sample – International Level Women TD
1	6.1 (21 strides)	6.0 (20 strides)	6.5 (23 strides)
2	9.8 (3.7)	9.8 (3.8)	11.1 (4.6)
3	13.6 (3.8)	13.6 (3.8)	15.7 (4.6)
4	17.4 (3.8)	17.5 (3.9)	20.3 (4.6)
5	21.3 (3.9)	21.4 (3.9)	25.0 (4.7)
200m	(23.0)	(23.1)	(27.0)
6	25.4 (4.1)	25.5 (4.1)	29.8 (4.8)
7	29.5 (4.1)	29.6 (4.1)	34.7 (4.9)
8	33.7 (4.2)	33.9 (4.3)	39.7 (5.0)
9	38.1 (4.4)	38.2 (4.3)	44.9 (5.2)
10	42.6 (4.5)	42.7 (4.5)	50.1 (5.2)
Run In	(5.2) (18 strides)	(4.9) (16 strides)	(5.9) (20 strides)
2nd 200m	(24.8)	(24.5)	(29.0)
Differential	1.8	1.4	2.0
Time	47.82	47.64	56.0
Total Strides	162	153	188

Akii-Bua strides: hurdles 3–5: 13 strides; hurdles 6–8: 14 strides; hurdles 9–10: 15 strides.

Moses strides: hurdles 5–10: 13 strides.

International Level Women strides: hurdles 3–7: 15 strides; hurdles 8–10: 17 strides.

From a report prepared for the BAAB by Sandy Ewen

21

The 400m hurdle final in the 1983 World Championships. Over 1.1 seconds separated the great Edwin Moses (47.50) from second place. The same interval separated second (No. 300: Harald Schmidt – FRG) from eighth. Moses' immaculate 10th hurdle clearance (loose shoe lace and all!) exemplifies his mastery of the event, even under extreme fatigue.

Stride pattern dictates the pace of the race. Differentials between the first and second 200m are: Moses 1.4, Akii-Bua 1.8, women 2.0 at best. (In reality, many women have closer to 5.0 seconds difference between the two). A realistic pace, use of touchdown charts and 200m differentials of less than 2.5 seconds must be worked into a successful race plan.

The usual 13 stride pattern used by men requires a transition or changedown phase around hurdle 4, 5, 6 or 7. As fatigue and oxygen debt set in, stride length shortens. A common practice is to run the first 5 or 6 hurdles at a set stride pattern of 13, 15 or 17 strides at which time 1 stride is added (14 or 16 strides) which requires alternating lead legs at subsequent hurdles. Another alternative is to add 2 strides for a 15 or 17 stride pattern which allows the athlete to continue hurdling with the same lead leg. The importance of the additional stride or two or more can be seen in Table 1-7. The change-over shifts from a longer stride to a quicker (but not choppy) one in an attempt to maintain the running rhythm. Minimum loss of speed and rhythm by maintaining a set stride pattern is the end goal.

Successful hurdlers are able to maintain initial rhythm to the first hurdle, between hurdles and through to the finish. For this reason, spatial awareness or the ability to judge or feel kinesthetically the body's speed and position relative to the hurdle clearances is an important aspect of 400m hurdling. All possible situations must be rehearsed. Head winds, tail winds, cross winds, lane draw, differences in track surfaces, weather conditions such as cold, heat and rain as well as the level and importance of the competition all have their implications on rhythm and can cause a great loss of speed if adjustments and corrections are not made immediately. The ability to lead with either leg, to sight the hurdle early in the attack phase, and to run the curves well must be rehearsed. An athlete may even have to move out in the lane (thereby adding running distance) to have a correct hurdle clearance. A poor hurdle clearance means correction before the next hurdle. The last 3 strides before and after clearance must be exact and consistent for every clearance with alterations being made between hurdles and not at them. Rhythm cannot be sacrificed to lack of care because the event allows no margin for error.

Race conditions will be less than ideal more often than they are ideal.
Successful hurdling comes from successful rehearsal in a variety of
situations.

Run In

Many positions in a race are determined in this last 40m. Special endurance training, good running mechanics and mental toughness produce the necessary final surge. The athlete should be aware of the number of strides to the finish line to dip at the proper moment.

The importance of Special Endurance 1 and 2 goes hand in hand with the importance of skill development. The limiting factor to Special Endurance is running technique: as the hurdler's fatigue increases in the latter parts of the race, weaknesses are compounded. Skill development and pace judgement are reflected in 200m differentials and touchdown times at various hurdles throughout the race. This information points out the strengths or weaknesses of the athlete's Special Endurance preparation. The speed of the first 200m has major implications for the final stages of the race. It has been seen that the last three Olympic gold medallists all had differentials of less than 2 seconds between the first and second halves of their race. This was not achieved by accident, but by constant careful attention to the strenuous preparation necessary.

Table 1-8 1983 World Championship Analysis
400m Hurdles — Men

Stride Pattern Used in Final

Height (cm)	Weight (kg)	Place	Name	Stride Pattern	Time
187	77.0	1	Edwin Moses (USA)	19 strides to H1, 13 to 10	47.50
185	82.0	2	Harald Schmid (FRG)	21 to H1, 13 to 7, 14 to 8, 15 to 9, 14 to 10	48.61
192	80.0	3	Aleksandr Kharlov (URS)	21 to H1, 13 to 10	49.03

Lead Legs

Lane	Name	H1	H2	H3	H4	H5	H6	H7	H8	H9	H10
2	Moses	L	L	L	L	L	L	L	L	L	L
7	Schmid	L	L	L	L	L	L	L	R	R	L
1	Kharlov	L	L	L	L	L	L	L	L	L	L
8	Nylander	L	L	L	L	L	R	L	L	L	L
6	Phillips	L	L	L	L	L	L	L	L	R	L
4	Lee	L	L	L	L	L	L	R	L	L	L
3	Dia Ba	L	L	L	L	L	L	R	L	R	L
5	Szparak	L	R	L	R	L	L	L	L	L	L

Touchdown Chart Analysis

Hurdle	Moses TD	Moses Difference	Schmid TD	Schmid Difference	Kharlov TD	Kharlov Difference
1	5.58		5.75		5.79	
2	9.29	(3.71)	9.24	(3.49)	9.58	(3.79)
3	13.21	(3.92)	13.24	(4.00)	13.75	(4.17)
4	16.79	(3.58)	—	—	—	—
5	20.71	(3.92)	20.93	—	21.80	—
6	24.63	(3.92)	24.93	(4.00)	25.80	(4.00)
7	28.80	(4.17)	28.81	(3.88)	29.97	(4.17)
8	32.97	(4.17)	33.48	(4.67)	34.47	(4.50)
9	37.43	(4.46)	38.31	(4.83)	39.05	(4.58)
10	41.97	(4.54)	43.02	(4.71)	43.76	(4.71)
Run In	5.53		5.59		5.27	
Time	47.50		48.61		49.03	

Canada's Andrea Page demonstrates the graceful technique of a top-class 400m hurdler.

Table 1-8 World Championship Analysis Helsinki 1983 – 400m Hurdles – Women

Stride Pattern Used in Final

Height (cm)	Weight (kg)	Place	Name	Stride Pattern	Time
171	61.3	1	Jekaterina Fessenko (URS)	23 strides to H1, 17 to 10	54.14
173	60.8	2	Anna Ambroziene (URS)	24 strides to H1, 16 to 7, 17 to 10	54.15
174	55.8	3	Ellen Fiedler (GDR)	23 to H1, 15 to 7, 16 to 9, 17 to 10	54.55

Touchdown Chart Analysis

Hurdle	Fessenko TD	Fessenko Difference	Ambroziene TD	Ambroziene Difference	Fiedler TD	Fiedler Difference
1	6.74		6.69		6.44	
2	11.30	(4.56)	11.05	(4.36)	10.52	(4.08)
3	15.48	(4.18)	15.31	(4.26)	14.65	(4.13)
4	19.90	(4.42)	19.57	(4.26)	18.87	(4.22)
5	24.32	(4.42)	24.08	(4.51)	23.34	(4.47)
6	28.99	(4.67)	28.65	4.57)	28.04	(4.70)
7	33.68	(4.69)	33.31	(4.66)	32.64	(4.60)
8	38.31	(4.63)	38.15	(4.84)	37.77	(5.13)
9	43.21	(4.90)	43.13	(4.98)	42.90	(5.13)
10	48.32	(5.11)	48.16	(5.03)	48.26	(5.36)
Run In	5.82		5.99		6.29	
Time	54.15		54.15		54.55	

(Taken from a report done by Gary Winkler Florida State University Lehre der Leichtathletik No. 34, 1983)

27

CHAPTER 2

THE SKILLS OF HURDLING

"... the body is educated to "feel" correct movements."

Mark McKoy (CAN) leads Thomas Munkelt (GDR) over the last hurdle in a heat of the World Championships in Helsinki, 1983. Also shown are Tim Soper (NZL-#596) and Mark Holton (GBR-#331).

OVERVIEW OF A TRAINING SYSTEM: THE 5 S'S

As can be seen in Table 2-1, a training system contains a multitude of elements. They may appear to be overwhelming in their complexity, but with a well-organized approach and the help of a knowledgeable, sensitive coach, all the components are put together in a successful quest for the athlete's goals.

The major components of a system are only five in number and can be conveniently referred to as **"The 5 S's"**: **Skill, Suppleness, Speed, Stamina and Strength.** "The 5 S's" will be referred to throughout subsequent chapters. The 5 S's are subject to three basic principles of training:

(1) Specificity
(2) Overload
(3) Reversibility

The implications of these principles will be explored in the discussion of each component and in the context of the overall design of a training programme.

This chapter will deal with the skill necessary for top class hurdling. Skill is not only used in the general use of "ability" or "adroitness", but also in a precise technical sense applied to three areas:

(1) the warm-up
(2) sprinting and hurdling
(3) starting.

SKILL

| Warm-up | Sprinting | Hurdling | Starting |

Table 2-1 Overview of a Training System

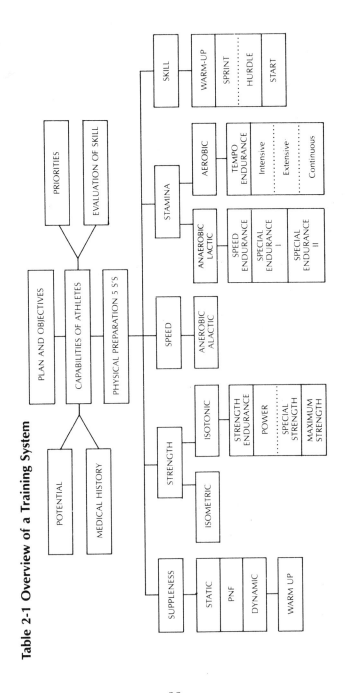

SUPPLENESS (FLEXIBILITY)

Used to maintain the alliteration of the 5 S's, the word "suppleness" is perhaps more commonly known as "flexibility". It is integrally involved with skill and is therefore dealt with in this chapter.

The words suppleness or flexibility are use to describe the range of movement in a joint or joints . It is of prime importance to hurdlers in the area of the hamstrings, hip, knee and ankle joints. In these events, flexibility contributes to muscle looseness, leg velocity, length of strides and sound technique.

Flexibility involves a muscle's myotatic or stretch reflex. Stretching a muscle activates nerve receptors in the muscle belly, which, in response, attempt to contract the stretched muscle. The faster and greater the degree of stretch, the stronger the reflex impulse to contract the muscle.

The components of flexibility can be broken down into 3 specific types:

(1) **Static flexibility** involves 'holding' a specific exercise for more than 20-30 seconds. If there is severe pain, it means the muscle is being stretched beyond its capacity ... STOP!! Warming up is to prevent injuries, not create them.

(2) **Proprioceptive Neuro-muscular Facilitation (PNF)** involves partner stretching where one partner applies pressure to a joint to its maximum (or near maximum) stretch. The athlete being stretched offers a resistance in the opposite direction of the initial force until the body part is back in its initial position. All stretching movements are done slowly and good partner cooperation is required.

(3) **Dynamic flexibility** involves repeated stretching movements with swinging, or other kinetic actions. Strongly correlated with speed of body movement, dynamic flexibility leads directly into skill or technique development where the body is educated to "feel" correct movements. This "feeling" is what is known as "kinesthesis". Kinesthesis brings together the technical skills of the event with the neuromus-

cular patterns necessary to stimulate correctly the muscle pairings. (These are made up of protagonist and antagonist muscles, respectively those which cause the desired action and those which return the moved joints to the initial position).

The teaching of the basic mechanics of sprinting and hurdling is often achieved through exercises such as "A" (high knees), "B" (leg extensions), "C" (hurdle trail leg drills). In these exercises, (dealt with later, Table 2-7) the key factors of the desired movement (hips tall, correct arm swing and active foot placement) are emphasized and become all part and parcel of dynamic flexibility.

The three fundamental principles of training apply to flexibility as to all components of a training programme: (1) **specificity**. Exercises must focus on specific joint actions and the demands of each event. (2) **overload**. Gains in flexibility occur when the limits of the existing range of movement are reached regularly, allowing new limits to be set; (3) **reversibility**. Improvements in flexibility will be lost if regular work is not maintained. The flexibility of an elite athlete begins to deteriorate after three days if some form of flexibility is not maintained … deterioration occurs as quickly as the gains. Since the body is built for speed and to do work, the implication is that flexibility gains come with use.

Table 2-2 101 Flexibility Exercises

34

Table 2-3 Sample Flexibility Circuits

The following sessions are designed specifically to enhance flexibility (which contributes to muscle looseness, leg velocity, length of stride, sound technique, injury prevention, warming up). Before doing sessions make sure the athlete has done some jogging and easy stretching (5-10 minutes). Exercises are to be done with a partner and held for 15-30 seconds (static and PNF series).

Session # 1

1. Sit with soles of feet together. Push thighs down with hands.

2. Put leg on hurdle (or partner). Face forward or sideways. Keep leg straight. Put head down to knee.

3. Lie on back with feet straddled. Try to close legs while partner keeps legs open. Close gradually.

    Lie on back with ankles crossed. Try to open legs while partner keeps them closed. Open gradually.

4. Hurdler's split options.

5. Inversion/Eversion: partner pulls toes in, out and down.

6.

Lie on back with one leg in air. Block other leg on ground and keep straight. Push leg towards head with resistance. Repeat 3 times.

7.

Kneel and lean backwards and hold.

Session #2

1.

Sitting with feet/legs under body. Lean back as far as possible.

2.

Straddle legs while sitting. Place head/shoulders on ground in front of body. Keep legs straight.

3.

Lie on stomach. Pick up thigh/leg as high as possible towards head. Partner may assist to lift leg up.

4.

Lie on stomach. Lift chest up(arch).

5.
Hurdler's split options

6.
Kneel. Alternate leg lifts for height above body. Leg can be bent or straight.

7.
Push up position. Keep feet together and walk up into arch position. Repeat down.

8. Standing with feet together. Bending over reach as far behind legs as possible.

9. High knee lift against a wall. Leg on ground lifts at ankle.

10. Standing. Lift 1 leg and hand for height.

Session # 3 (P.S. Drills)

A-skip, A-sprint, B-skip, bounding, A-skip, bum kicks (10-20m only).

SKILL DEVELOPMENT
IN THE WARM-UP

It is the author's position that the vast majority of athletes, whether novice or international, are negligent in warming up for general and specific training sessions. Too often, warm-up procedures are non-structured, and fail to rehearse the specifics of the event. It is an area which will invariably repay our attention if we as coaches are looking for ways to maximize performance.

Warming up basically reduces the number of muscles that may become injured and strained. Elasticity and relaxation of the running muscles increases, as well as reaction and movement times. Moreover, it is critical to warm up the mind as well as the body. Group warm-ups and teaching of correct procedures are very valuable in the pre-competitive periods but should lead to individualized and independent warm-ups during competition.

Three examples of well-structured warm-up procedures will be used to illustrate the principles.

Mach Warm-up

The most common warm-up used in Canada is the "Mach" style (Table 2-4) which is capable of many variations as required. It was introduced to the country's coaches in the early 70's by Head Coach Gerard Mach as a result of many years of refinement with sprinters in his native Poland, where he was Head Coach during the 50's and 60's, the Golden Age of Polish sprinting supremacy.

Table 2-4 Mach Warm-up

Part I:	(done in training shoes)
	(i) 3 × 50m (100h, 110h) or 3 × 100m (400 h) easy jog on grass followed by shoulder rotations (5mins for loose upper body)
	(ii) 3 × 50 plus lower body flexibilty
	(iii) 3 × 50 plus skill (A's, B's, C's)
Part 2:	(done in spikes)
	Accelerations over 30–40m with the possibility of some block starts and with or without hurdles

Continuous Warm-up

The second example of warm-up procedure has been successfully used by the author and others to integrate kinetic flexibility exercises. It is known as The Continuous Warm-up and can include different exercise components varying between general preparation in the off-season to specific preparation in the competition season. Indeed, a combination of both can be used year-round. (Table 2-5).

Using the continuous warm-up method, it takes at least 15 minutes to get an equilibrium between core and peripheral body temperatures. Women may take less time since they are more flexible and have less muscle. The continuous movement (jogging) along with kinetic flexibility exercises that precede a workout, allow for a mental and physical adjustment while raising the body temperature. In the winter, this warm-up may take 20 to 25 minutes, while in the summer 30 to 35 minutes, done slower with fewer exercises. It is a **non-stop** session and has the advantage of needing only 50–60 metres, making it suitable for use where facilities are limited.

Table 2-5 Continuous Warm-up

1   4 × 50m easy jog (turnaround every 50m)
2   jog backwards 50m and jog 50m
3   jog 50m changing direction and jog backwards 50m
4   jog 2 × 50m slowly bending to touch ground (3 point start) and gradually accelerate 10 to 15 metres
5   jog 50m doing high knee lifts as you feel (A's at a skip) alternating legs. Jog 50m
6   jog 50m doing leg extensions (B's at a skip) as you feel alternating legs. Jog 50m
7   easy jog for 50m bending over to touch toes as you go
8   skipping 50m (no rope needed) with arms swinging
9   walk 50m swinging arms forwards
10 walk 50m swinging arms backwards
11 walk 50m fast swinging arms fast forwards
12 jog 50m trippling (ankle drive drill)
13 jog 50m with ankle hops (extensions/driving) (both ankles, left, right, side to side)
14 jog 50m doing alternate knee lifts (A's) to the front and then to the side (switch legs) as you feel
15 repeat 14 with emphasis on ankle drive
16 jog 50m doing cross steps (running sideways) with arms crossed in front of body and alternating direction of cross step
17 walk several times 50m doing various flexibility movements: alternate toe touching (gently dynamic), hip circles (twists), ankle extensions (achilles stretch), groin stretch (lunge position) – a total of 10 repetitions per exercise are necessary to get the desired effect
18 walk several times 50m doing event specific flexibility exercises using a partner, equipment or a support; hurdle lead leg drills on a wall, free leg swings forward and sideways (straight and bent leg) while leaning against a wall, various hurdling stretch positions while sitting (gently dynamic), leg swings forward to kick hands in front of body (there is an endless choice to suit needs)
19 sprint drills 40 × (high knee lifts, trail leg action, leg extensions) (actually A,C and B Mach exercises) done over 20m distances with a walkback recovery. Start slowly and get more dynamic
20 jog 2 × 50m each including 6 times easy starting positions and accelerations
21 2 × 50m easy acceleration
22 2 × 50m controlled and smooth acceleration (95%)

23 40m acceleration, hold speed for 20m and then
    relax
24 repeat 23 emphasizing frequency and "fast hands"
25 hurdle event specific drills: runs over 1 to 4 hurdles
    using 4 stride pattern with walkback recovery.
    (Fewer exercises, longer time for warming up and
    more recovery are necessary in the competition
    phase of this continuous warm-up. The warm-up
    ends 30 minutes before competition.)

   One may use as many exercises as desired (starting with
general and working to specific) provided that they are
effective at speed while using a full range of motion. Dynamic flexibility must relate to a given event's technique
while building on the laws of specificity, overload and
reversibility. It has been the author's observation that, as
competition approaches, more recovery is incorporated
between exercises. This often includes the shaking of the
leg muscles in an attempt to enhance muscle relaxation.

Warm-Up Procedures of the GDR Women's Hurdlers

   The third illustration is an actual example of warm-up
used by one of the best prepared women's hurdling programmes in the world. The GDR coaches and athletes
leave nothing to chance in their quest for medal
performances.
   At the 1983 World Championships in Helsinki, the author observed a total of 15 very sequenced and articulated
warm-up series, which were basically of the same design.
Although nothing new or startling is incorporated, these
warm-ups do have a direct correlation with the results
seen on the track. Simply, the warm-up plan does have a
sequence, does follow basic physiological principles and
does the job ...

The results of the warm-up procedures described in these pages! East Germany's Bettine Jahn (right lane) and Kirsten Knabe (left lane) about to win gold and silver respectively in the 1983 World Championships with times of 12.35 and 12.42 respectively.

No. 190 (Shirley Strong – GBR) and No. 495 (Benita Fitzgerald – USA) were the only non-East Europeans in the final, finishing 5th (12.78) and 8th (12.99) respectively. Their turn came in the 1984 Los Angeles Olympics: Fitzgerald won the gold (12.84) and Strong the silver (12.88).

Table 2-6 Warm-Up procedures of the GDR Women Hurdlers

1st IAAF World Championships, Helsinki, 1983

PART I (total time 20 minutes)

This initial series of exercises involves a tremendous amount of dynamic flexibility (swinging, bouncing type movements) that were done gradually and easily. Every body part, expecially joints, were continuously rotated and flexed in a specific pattern. No static (held) movements were observed in any of the 15 warm-ups.

1   easy jog on cinder lane inside warm-up track,
    6 × 100m turn-arounds on the straight (very little
    warming up was done on the track)
2   12 × easy ankle stretches (bouncing in nature)
3   standing alternate toe touches (bouncing
    movement), walk after a few reps
4   5 × side steps facing different directions, with a few
    knee lift exercises
5   ankle extensions with bent knee while walking
    100m, with easy jog
6   "bum kicks" with jog over a 100m distance
7   upper body arm circles (10 reps)
8   hip (waist) circles (10 reps)

9　ankle stretches (bouncing movement) in lunge position
10　achilles stretches (leaning against an object) (10 reps)
11　5 × knee lifts to front of body and to side of body
12　arm circles (rotations) while bent over and to the ground
13　leg shaking (standing and sitting)
14　hurdle stretch with trail leg to inside of crotch (bouncing action)
15　leg shaking
16　hurdle stretch with bouncing movements lead knee, middle and trail leg, leg shaking and then repeated with other leg (alternated)
17　6 × sit, pick up leg into air and straighten knee, leg shaking
18　9 × lead leg swinging drill over side of hurdle
19　5 × stationary fast legs and short arm punch
20　leg shaking

PART II (in spikes; 40 minutes)

This second part of the warm up was very specific to the exact skills of the sprint hurdle event. All rehearsing was done with exactness to minimize any possible deviation or error.

1　50m acceleration on track with a walk back to start
2　50m acceleration; stand up start with increase in speed after 20m (emphasis on short step frequency and fast hands … extremely fast)
3　2 × 30m falling type start (hands in front of body and fast frequency)
4　20m falling start (quick hands and feet)
5　easy run over 1 hurdle with a walk back recovery
6　4 hurdles placed for 5 strides between hurdles (quick hands emphasis, fast downward action off hurdle, fast leg turnover)
7　2 minute rest
8　4 hurdles with 5 strides between (using exaggerated running motion)
9　4 hurdles with 5 strides (run off last hurdle hard; trail leg drops quickly after each hurdle; fast leg turnover)
10　sweats and rain pants put on; set up block using measuring tape
11　sweats off; start over 1 hurdle
12　start over 1 hurdle, hurdle 2 flat on track but run over using 5 strides
13　start over 2 hurdles with emphasis on "fast hands" and pulling of trail leg (5 strides between hurdles)
14　departure for competition stadium

The entire warm-up procedure takes exactly one hour and ends exactly 30 minutes before race time.

PART III (competition stadium)
1   3 × hurdle 1 using blocks
2   lots of leg shaking (while sitting)
3   start over 2 hurdles (5 strides between hurdles)
4   RACE (Jahn 12.35; Knabe 12.42)(1st and 2nd).

The warm-up procedure, timing and sequencing had minimal alterations between rounds. The GDR women were there for one purpose ... to produce in the finals.

"Results speak for themselves". Just prior to the sprint hurdles for women, the author witnessed the same preciseness and rehearsal by two other women from the GDR, Marita Koch and Marlies Gohr, who also placed first and second in the 100m final.

SKILL IN SPRINTING AND HURDLING

Prospective hurdlers who have good speed and flexibility should be immediately introduced to the fundamental movements of sprinting and hurdling. It is not a complex procedure but is accomplished through a series of simple exercises carefully arranged in a progression so as to facilitate the acquisition of the skill components of sprinting and hurdling actions.

To Canadians, the "Mach" exercises for sprinting and hurdling present important components of a system that is recognized across the country. The purpose of this section is to explain them and the concepts behind them.

The goals of the skill exercises are:

(1) to isolate and combine a joint (or joints) to the specificity of sprinting and hurdling

(2) to maintain and improve these skills with continuous development in speed, flexibility, strength and speed endurance (rhythm).

The diagrams of the "A", "B" and "C" exercises are presented as Table 2-6. They each are done in a three-fold progression: marching, skipping and running. They can be done with and without hurdles. A simple explanation and key phrases are under each diagram.

The progression starts with "A" exercises (high knee lift) using one leg only. Stress the actions of a high knee lift, hips tall, stretched tall, aligned arm position and an active landing on the ball of the foot.

Once an athlete is able to do this correctly with one leg, he/she should try the other leg. When each leg is able to do the action correctly, the athlete may begin to "march" using both legs alternately. When the march is mastered, an athlete may progress to the skipping and running forms. "B"'s follow the same learning sequence. (Combinations of A's and B's can also be done with each leg doing either an A or B action.)

Throughout these progressions, it is important to remember that sprinting and hurdling involve learning through kinesthesis — teaching the body to feel certain positions. The learning and perfection of skills must be done correctly, efficiently and "perfectly". Doing skills incorrectly means repetition of error. Therefore, STOP, if this happens. Each skill must be correct before moving to the next. To correct skills learned incorrectly may take months or years.

Table 2-7 Mach Exercises

A's
(High knee lift)
A march (1 or 2 legs)
A skip (1 or 2 legs)
A sprint (1 or 2 legs)

High knee lifts (single or alternate) can be done in marching, skipping, or running forms. Stress the perfection of the exercise, hip tall, stretched tall body position, active landing of feet, short and straight arm swing. Done without hurdles or over the side or hurdles.

B's
B march (1 or 2 legs)
B skip (1 or 2 legs)
B sprint (1 or 2 legs)
Combinations of A's, B's, A + B march
A + B skip-use both legs
A + B sprint

High knee lift with foreleg extension (single or alternate legs) done in marching, skipping or running forms. Stress same technique as in A's. Done without hurdles or over the side of hurdles. The emphasis is on the "pulling down" of the leg after the foreleg extension, not the kicking out of the extension itself.

C's

(trail leg action)
C march (1 or 2 legs)
C skip (1 or 2 legs)
C sprint (1 or 2 legs)
Combinations with Trail
(lead leg and trail leg)
A + C march, skip, sprint
A + B march, skip, sprint

This is the trail leg action used in hurdling only. The exercise is done in marching, skipping and running forms over trail leg side of hurdle. Stress hips tall, tucking trail heel to buttocks, pulling trail heel off hurdle, pawing action of lead arm and running off hurdle with trail leg.

As with the A and B exercises, the trail leg drills start with the simple march form, progress to the skip form and finally the running form over the side of the hurdle.

"B" action   **"A" action**

High lead leg action on take-off

The introduction of "C" or trail leg hurdling exercises is not so simple. The correct mechanical action will have to be taught. A coach must put an athlete through a vigorous flexibility programme of trail leg exercises before introducing the hurdle.

Action over Hurdle

When used for hurdlers, the A and B exercises are done over the side of the hurdle – one leg will clear the hurdle while the other will do its action beside the hurdle. The same teaching progressions and emphasis are used as when no hurdles are present. Begin with the simplest forms of marching A's, progress to skipping and finally the running forms over the side of the hurdle. Make sure both legs are done on each side of the hurdle. B's (lower leg extensions) follow similarly.

"C" exercises over the hurdle involve the lead leg stepping beyond the side of the hurdle with the trail leg then clearing only half the hurdle. This must be done several hundred times in the initial learning period to perfect the correct trail leg action and will be closely monitored even as the athlete progresses.

Finally the drills are done over the middle of the hurdle with the complete hurdling action perfected.

For developing hurdling, the height of the hurdle will vary with the skill of the athlete; lower hurdles should be used for beginners. The following notes may be useful:

(1) To introduce skill exercises use only one or two hurdles. As skill improves the number of hurdles may be increased.
(2) Advanced hurdlers will do 8 to 12 hurdles placed 2 to 3 metres apart using 1 step between hurdles. Emphasis is on perfection and a rhythmic cadence.
(3) Once all this basic skill has been accomplished place the hurdles 4 metres apart and have the athletes run over the side of the hurdles using 1 stride using either the lead or trail leg.
(4) The hurdles can then be placed at reduced spacings using the same drills.

Skill exercises can be done under two conditions to rehearse totally different aspects of a race:

(1) **Power Speed:** refers to doing skill exercises up to 20 metres or less than 10 repetitions or less than 10 seconds. This type of work has an important effect in the initial parts of the sprint races. Emphasis is on the speed of correct execution.
(2) **Strength Endurance:** refers to doing skill exercises for more than 20 metres or more than 10 repetitions or more than 10 seconds. This type of work is very beneficial in the later part of the hurdle races. Emphasis is on the rhythm of correct execution under fatigue.

As an athlete progresses, Power Speed and Strength Endurance exercises can be done with added resistance such as a weight belt or sandbag. (See also Appendix A).

47

Other drills to develop skill in hurdling

Face the side of the hurdle. Lead foot clears back and forth over the edge of the hurdle. Key on the foot. Keep the toe up. Keep body tall.

Anisimova Drills (USSR)

'A' skip crossing over side of hurdle.

Wall attack drills use the lead leg and begin from a high 'A' action which attacks the wall as the athlete falls towards it. The toes are 'cocked' up and the opposite hand also attacks the wall.

Wall Attack

High A with foot and hand attack.

This drill is designed to rehearse 'tall' hips and ankle strength. Hop holding lead leg up (A or B position). Once this is perfected step over a hurdle and bring trail leg over into an 'A' position.

Karate Kid Kick

Karate stance + hop + kick
(and reverse legs)

Trail leg mechanics can be perfected by standing beside the hurdle and skipping with trail leg clearing every 3rd stride or on every stride. Forms used can be march, skip or running forms.

Continuous trail legs (USSR)

Skip 1, 2, 3 then trail clears. Run on spot 1, 2, 3 + clearance. 1 step skip + trail clearance.

Lead leg is held in an 'A' position. Athlete hops up to hurdle with lead held up and steps over hurdle. Trail leg is also pulled over hurdle into 'A' held position. Repeat with other lead leg up to 5-8 hurdles.

Calvesi Drills (Italy)

'A' hop over hurdles.

Held 'A'

Jog with both hands held at chest height. While jogging drive lead knee into hands (ie. Right knee into right hand). Once this is done repeat with each knee being driven simultaneously into the hands to a 1-2 count. Once accomplished repeat with a slight body lean. Finally, repeat entire action over a hurdle ... ensure the 1-2 knee action, with body lean and cocked foot occur.

Ross Drills (USA)

Double knee hit/slap.
(Fast 1-2 knee strike)

Dynamic Drills

Dynamic drills involve fast movements which can be designed to simulate any desired part of the hurdle action.

Elastic or surgical tubing can be used to enhance hurdle skills.

cable

Take off drills to enhance ankle drive.

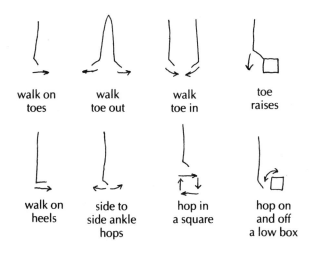

| walk on toes | walk toe out | walk toe in | toe raises |

| walk on heels | side to side ankle hops | hop in a square | hop on and off a low box |

SKILL IN THE STARTING BLOCKS

An efficient start allows an athlete to accelerate out of the block and reach maximum speed as soon as possible. The starting position must be comfortable and mechanically correct in both the 'on your marks' and 'set' positions to allow the hurdler to move the arms first and fast into the sprint action, and secondly, to get maximum impulse (force × time) from driving off the blocks. The start is an integral part of the whole hurdle race, not a separate skill.

The "medium" start is generally held to be superior over both the "bunch (short)" and "elongated" starting positions. It provides the 'compromise' needed to allow for a fast acceleration of the body's centre of gravity, good forward body lean and maximum impulse. The start itself has two components.

Firstly is the reaction time to the gun. I.A.A.F. rules state that on the command 'set' all competitors shall "at once and without delay assume their full and final set position. Failure to comply after a reasonable time shall constitute a false start." The hurdler's concentration should be on the forthcoming motion rather than on the sound of the gun. The gun simply releases the actions of sprinting. To improve the excitability of motor neurons and the synchronous firing of the motor units, the coach should stress fast limb movement being "released" by the gun. Reaction times may vary between .12 secs (world class) to .225 secs (novice). It may be rehearsed and improved with specifically designed exercises.

Secondly is movement time and acceleration from the blocks. The technical skills of starting should be learned at slower speeds before progressing to maximum speed.

Training for maximum speed requires a complete warm-up with no fatigue present for improved neuronal programming and injury-free preparation. It is not the purpose here to discuss the mechanical complexities of the sprint start which are adequately dealt with elsewhere. Nevertheless, the key factors above affect the skill of the start and thus cannot be overlooked.

(1) To develop the greatest possible forward lean (42–45 degrees) and maximum acceleration of the body's centre of gravity, a compromise between the horizontal and vertical force components must be made. The horizontal component must be greater to overcome the body's inertia and to resist the vertical component, ie. the tendency to stand up. Lean is proportional to the strength and acceleration ability of the athlete. Acceleration is greatest when the forward lean is the greatest.

(2) All movements initiated on the gun must be forcefully carried out through a full range of movement to get maximum impulse. Incorrect application of force through a full range of movement is one of the greatest common errors of starting. Although initially there is equal drive from both feet against the blocks, the rear leg when vigorously driving forward from the blocks creates an equal and opposite reaction backwards. Only by full extension of the lower leg complex (hip, knee, ankle joints) against the front block can inertia be overcome and maximum impulse be achieved. This summation of forces (when correctly applied from large body parts to smaller ones), allows for many other technical components of the start to correctly fall into place and occur naturally.

(3) Fighting for block speed only creates unwanted tension. The individual capabilities and limitations of each athlete such as strength, flexibility, skill and muscle type are limiting factors imposed on the achievement of maximum performance. Only by rehearsing starting skills can neuromuscular responses, coordination and the correct learning process be implanted in the body's neuromuscular memory system.

It must be accepted that many basic components of a good start can be learned while others are limited by an athlete's physiological make-up. Nevertheless, the following drills are specifically designed to help fulfill the requirements of correct and efficient sprint starting.

Table 2-8 Medicine Ball Exercises for Starting Skill

These exercises are designed to assist forward lean, full leg extension and range of motion, maximum impulse and basic skill of an efficient start without using the blocks. Athletes either lean forward or squat and throw the medicine ball forward, extending as far as possible before releasing the ball. After catching the body weight on the hands, the regular start position is taken and an easy run forward follows. The drills are extended one step further with the ball being thrown forward and the athlete follows quickly, using the basic skills of starting: active foot placement, long, vigorous arm swing and forward lean.

Lean ♦ Fall ♦ Start ♦ Run

Lean ♦ Run

Squat ♦ Fall ♦ Start ♦ Run

Squat ♦ Run

Standing Throw   Run

Punch Drill

Punch   Catch

SKILL EVALUATION

Hurdling is a faultless sprint over barriers. The entire science of hurdling must be exercised and evaluated to maximize one's performance — an aspect thoroughly understood where the event is seriously studied.

A Hurdling Skill Diagnostic Sheet

Table 2-9 is one form of a diagnostic sheet which can be used to evaluate a single hurdle clearance or a series of clearances. Few coaches have access to specialized cinematography equipment and therefore must rely on their eyes to make some type of evaluation of their athletes against the best hurdling technique and biomechanics. This list is not intended to replace other scientific or subjective methods which may be used. It is put forward simply as a guide to assist the coach and to reinforce the contention that the process of diagnostic evaluation is indispensable.

Coaching Observation Point

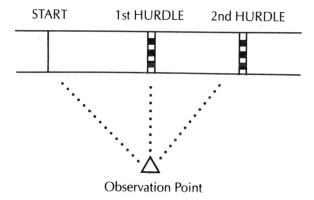

Observation Point

Table 2-9 Hurdling Diagnostic Sheet

STAGE OF RACE	ACTION	EVALUATION POINT

Sprinting Technique	Drive Phase	Extension at hip
		              at knee
		              at ankle

		Forward motion of hips of centre of gravity
	Recovery Phase	Knee lift
		Position of centre of gravity
	Skill development	A exercise – Knee lift – Straight supporting leg
		B exercise – Knee extension – Straight supporting leg
		Posture – Alignment of arms – Coordination of arms
Start and Sprint approach to first hurdle	Starting technique	Blocks – Spacing – Measurements to startline

		"On your marks" – Foot placement
		              – Hand placement
		              – Total body
		                position
		              – Comfort

		"Set" – Knee angle
		         – Hip height
		         – Foot placement
		         – Head position
		         – Body position

	Sprint approach to first hurdle	Block clearance – Low heel recovery
		                  – Accelerating centre
		                    of gravity

		Position – Balanced position – Eye focus

		Strides – Measurement of
		              progressive lengthening
		        – Balance

		Transition to – Stride transition
		hurdle clearance – Speed of approach
		              – Arm alignment
		              – Running plane of
		                motion

Hurdle take off	Lead leg	Basic skill – Execution of "A" action – Execution of "B" action
		Straight line action in sagittal plane
		Flexibility – Knee angle – Thigh above horizontal

		Angular velocity – At hip
		                – At knee
		                – At ankle

		Leg position – Knee (bent or stretched
		                before hurdle)
		          – Length
		          – Leads attack

STAGE OF RACE	ACTION	EVALUATION POINT
Hurdle take off	Trail Leg	Basic skill – Execution of "C" action
		Foot placement at take off
		Flexibility – "Stretched tall" position 　　　　　– Extension at hip 　　　　　– Extension at knee 　　　　　– Extension at ankle
		Leg position – Begins action when 　　　　　lead leg is at or over 　　　　　hurdle
	Arms & Shoulders	Basic action　– Single, 1½ or double 　　　　　– Plane of motion
		Position　　　– Shoulders square 　　　　　– Elbow angle 　　　　　– Balance of lead and trail 　　　　　　arms 　　　　　– Body lean
	Total Action	Distance from hurdle – measurement
		Path of centre of gravity
		Position – Stretched tall 　　　　　– Balance and coordination
Hurdle Clearance	Lead Leg	Sagittal plane of motion
		Angular velocity of entire leg
		Straight or flexed over barrier
	Trail Leg	Horizontal plane of motion
		Position – Rotation at hip 　　　　　– Angle of knee 　　　　　– Heel and toe
		Action off hurdle – Knee or foot leads 　　　　　– Balance 　　　　　– Final position
	Total Action	Length of total clearance-measurement Distance to take off to hurdle – measurement Distance of landing from hurdle – measurement
		Parabolic curve of centre of gravity
		Position – "Pawing" of arms 　　　　　– Body lean 　　　　　– Hip moving forward 　　　　　– Balance and coordination
		Athlete's feel
Action from hurdle	Lead leg	Sagittal plane of action
		Position – Stretched tall 　　　　　– Foot action (flat or active)
	Trail leg	First stride from hurdle – Length 　　　　　– Speed
		Position – Flexibility 　　　　　– Foot action (flat or active)
	Total action	Centre of gravity – Position 　　　　　– Moving forward

STAGE OF RACE	ACTION	EVALUATION POINT

Action from hurdle		Position – Hips
		        – Rotations
		        – Balance

		Athlete's feel
Whole Race Analysis	Hurdles 1-5	Touchdown times
		Rhythm
	Hurdles 6-10	Touchdown times
		Rhythm
	Last hurdle to finish	Landing from hurdle 10
		Number of strides to finish
		Dip at line
	Overall	Touchdown times
		Rhythm
		Athlete's feel

Curve of centre of gravity

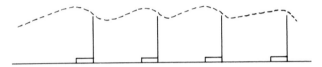

Rhythm

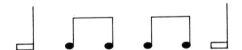

56

Elite Film Analysis

It has been mentioned that few coaches have regular access to film analysis of their athletes. Where it is available, however, the field of high speed cinematography has led to greater improvements, more scientific verification and the detailed information necessary for coaches to look at their event with a finer eye. The expertise of the coaches' eye need not be the only means for error correction. The following analysis gives a coach "food for thought" as an example of the necessary information to "see" and correct errors at an advanced level.

The information in Table 2-9 was tabulated by Kodak Sweden for three runs of Ann Louise Skogland in her quest for a 100m hurdle time of 12.60. The guide indicates times that are necessary to run this time with the camera providing a specific breakdown of contact times, touchdown times, flight times and distances for take-off and landing between hurdles. A close look at this data gave her coaches such valuable information as: (1) more speed over and between hurdles is necessary; (2) the take-off stride before the hurdle (3rd stride) is too long and Ann Louise's contact on the ground is too great. A shorter stride before takeoff is necessary. (3) Hip position over the hurdles must be higher to allow for a faster clearance as well as faster flight times.

It is worth noting that such analysis can have far-reaching consequences when properly used. As a result of this and other data, the decision was made that Ann Louise might be more suited to the 400m hurdles. While remedial technique work was being done, she embarked at the same time onto a period of preparation which ultimately led her to the 400m hurdles final in the 1984 Olympic Games. Here she was involved in a thrilling three-way finish which left her in fifth place, just two one-hundredths of a second from a bronze medal.

Table 2-10 Film Analysis – Ann Louise Skoglund

Best 100m hurdle time 13.25
Goal 100m hurdle time 12.60

Best 100m time
Estimated 100m needed to reach hurdle goal
11.70
11.45

	Needed for goal 12.60	1st run			2nd run			3rd run		
		H1	H2	H3	H1	H2	H3	H1	H2	H3
Clearance Time over hurdle (secs)	0.28	–	0.305	0.290	0.300	0.315	0.305	–	0.300	0.300
Contact Time (on ground) for each stride (secs)										
Landing Stride	0.10	0.115	0.105	0.105	0.115	0.105	0.110	0.115	0.100	0.110
1st Stride	0.12	–	0.130	0.110	–	0.125	–	–	0.130	0.125
2nd Stride	0.12	–	0.110	–	–	0.130	–	–	–	–
3rd (take off) Stride	0.11	0.135	0.140	–	0.135	0.125	–	0.140	0.145	–
Recovery Time (off ground) for each stride (secs)										
1st Stride	0.09	–	0.100	0.100	–	0.100	–	–	0.095	0.102
2nd Stride	0.13	–	0.160	–	–	0.135	–	–	–	–
3rd (take off) Stride	0.10	–	0.105	–	–	0.101	–	–	–	–
Total touch down time between hurdles (secs)	1.05	1.150	1.140	–	1.165	1.130	–	1.160	1.135	–
Speed (metres per second)	8.09	7.39	7.45	–	7.24	7.52	–	7.32	7.49	–
Total clearance distance over hurdle (m)	3.10	–	2.79	–	–	2.70	–	–	2.82	–
Take off distance to hurdle (m)	2.00	–	1.77	–	–	2.70	–	–	2.82	–
Landing distance from hurdle (m)	1.10	–	1.02	–	–	1.14	–	–	0.99	–

Testing for the Hurdle Events

For a coach, identifying, evaluating and programming those with potential talent in the hurdle events is an endless task. How are those with potential in the hurdle events identified? How are progress and yearly development evaluated and measured? How available is medical and university personnel to assist? How can those with limited resources attempt to emulate the Eastern block countries with their systematic programme, supported by medical and research staff, specifically designed to produce Olympic medallists?

Many of the current talent assessment tests such as percent body fat measurements, jumps decathlon, circuit training tests, anthropometric data, and detailed blood analysis are too general and lack the specificity needed to evaluate hurdlers. "Simple" and "specific" are key words here. Simple means that all coaches and athletes must be able to use some form of testing at all levels of performance. Specific means that the tests must deal directly with hurdlers' needs and problems.

The tests proposed in Table 2-11 for evaluating hurdlers are in no way exhaustive nor need they all be used at every test session. Before deciding which tests are to be given, the phase of training, individual training needs and injury possibilities and problems must all be taken into consideration. Monthly test results are recorded, graphed and evaluated to show strengths and weaknesses. A typical recording sheet is shown as Table 2-12.

These tests are designed to complement, not replace other forms of hurdle evaluation. The use of touchdown times, standard flexibility tests, time trials over various hurdle combinations and time differentials between the flat sprint races and hurdle races can be very useful. There are no tables or charts to compare results from the above tests to other hurdlers but like racing results, data from these tests can show progress over the year for the members of each coaching group.

Table 2-11 Hurdle Tests

SPEED:
1) 30m sprint: Standing start. No command. Start timing when the back foot leaves the ground until the torso crosses the finish line. 2 attempts.
2) 50m sprint: Same procedure as 30m sprint. 2 attempts.

HURDLE SKILL:
3) 10 hurdles placed 2m apart at 76cm (30″) height for women or 91.5cm (36″) for men. The athlete must skip over the side of the hurdle using 1 step between hurdles, first using lead leg, secondly using trail leg, and thirdly over the middle using the entire hurdling action. Start timing when the back foot leaves the ground on the 1st hurdle until it contacts the ground after the last hurdle clearance. 2 attempts.
4) 10 hurdles placed 3.5 to 4.0m apart at 76cm (women) or 91.5cm (men). The athlete is allowed a 6 to 8m approach to run over the 10 hurdles using 1 running stride between. Same timing procedure as #3. 2 attempts.

SPECIAL HURDLING TESTS:
5) 50m hurdles: 4 hurdles placed 8.30m apart at 84cm (33″) height and 13m approach to the 1st hurdle for women. (Men: 13.72m to 1st hurdle, 9m apart, 91.5cm height). Same timing procedure as 30m sprint. 2 attempts.
6) Run over 5 hurdles: same specifications as 50m hurdles with another hurdle added. Start timing when the back foot leaves the ground at the start until the lead leg touches the ground (touchdown time) after the 5th hurdle clearance. 60 second recovery and repeat. Time for 2 runs added together and recorded. 2 attempts. Or 5 × 5 hurdle run: same specifications and timing procedure as run over 5 hurdles. Time for 5 hurdle runs added together and recorded. 1 attempt.
7) 400m hurdle test: run over 5 hurdles with 5 stride rhythm as follows for men: 13.72m to 1st hurdle, 13m between hurdles, 91.5cm height, total run 70m. (Women: 13m to 1st hurdle, 76cm height, 11m between hurdles, total run 70m). Same timing procedure as 30m sprint. 2 attempts.

ENDURANCE:

8) Special Endurance: 300m run: same timing procedures as 30m sprint. After 200m a second watch is used to time last 100m of the 300m. Both times are recorded. 1 attempt.

9) Optional: Aerobic Endurance 12 minute run. Total metres run are recorded. 1 attempt. (Not recommended for 100/110m hurdlers).

BOUNDING:

10) 50m bounding for 100/110m hurdlers: start from stride position and time when back foot leaves ground until torso crosses the finish line. Athlete attempts to cover distance in as few strides as possible and the least possible time.

Record: (i) number of total bounds to cover the distance.

(ii) time required to complete distance. 2 attempts.

100m bounding for 400m hurdlers: Same procedures as 50m bounding.

Table 2-12 Testing Record Chart

TEST		Session 1 Date:	Session 2 Date:
SPEED 1) 30m Sprint	1st trial 2nd trial		
2) 50m Sprint	1st trial 2nd trial		
HURDLE SKILL 3) 10 hurdle drill i) lead leg	1st trial 2nd trial		
ii) trail leg	1st trial 2nd trial		
iii) total action	1st trial 2nd trial		
4) 10 hurdle run	1st trial 2nd trial		
RHYTHM TESTS 5) 50m hurdles	1st trial 2nd trial		
6) 2 × 5 hurdles	1st trial 2nd trial total time		
5 × 5 hurdles	1st trial 2nd trial total time		
7) 400m hurdle test (5 hurdles, 5 stride rhythm)	1st trial 2nd trial		
ENDURANCE 8) 300m run	1st trial last 100m		
9) 12 minute run	1st trial		
BOUNDING 10) 50m Bound (100/110 hurdlers)	1st trial 2nd trial	time no of bounds time no of bounds	
100m Bound (400 hurdlers)	1st trial 2nd trial	time no of bounds time no of bounds	

SUMMARY

The total puzzle of sprinting and hurdling now begins to come together. Once skill preparation has been perfected under simple conditions, the athlete is ready to move forward to Speed and Speed Endurance (Special Endurance in Mach's terminology) over hurdles. The link between the skills and the ability to perform them under varying conditions of fatigue will be explored in the next chapter.

CHAPTER 3

THE HURDLING BODY

*"To maintain muscular activity...
the immediate production and replacement
of ATP is necessary"*

Gwen Wall (CAN) en route to a 4th place in the 400m
hurdles in the Commonwealth Games, Edinburgh 1986.

CHAPTER AT A GLANCE

INTRODUCTION
Overview
ATP – The Source of Muscular Energy

THE ANAEROBIC ALACTIC ENERGY SYSTEM
The Role of Creatine Phosphate
An Overview of Speed
Speed Training
Motor Performance & Speed
Sequencing Speed

THE ANAEROBIC LACTIC ENERGY SYSTEM
The Process of Glycolysis
Speed Endurance
Overview
Speed Endurance in the 100m Hurdle Events: the Concept of Rhythm
Sequencing Rhythm
Touchdown Analysis – 100m/110m hurdles
Special Endurance I
Special Endurance 2
Touchdown Analysis – 400m hurdles

THE AEROBIC ENERGY SYSTEM
The Role of Oxygen
Training the Aerobic System
Tempo Endurance
Hills

SUMMARY

Table 3-1 Energy System Overview

Energy System	Anaerobic Alactic (ATP + CP)	Anaerobic Lactic (Glycolysis)			(Shared Lactic/ Aerobic)	Aerobic (Krebs Cycle)	
Component	Speed	Speed Endurance	Special Endurance 1	Special Endurance 2	Tempo (intensive)	Tempo (extensive)	Tempo (continuous)
Intensity	95-100%	95-100%	95-100%	95-100%	80-90+%	60-80%	40-60%
Time	7 sec	7-20 sec	20-40sec	40sec-2min	40sec-2min	40sec-2min	2mins +
Distance	20-60m	80-150m	150-300m	300-600m	up to 600m	up to 600m	long
Application to 110/100H	H1-5	H6-10					
Application to 400mH		H1-3	H4-8	H8-10			
European Equivalent Terminology	Alactic Power	Alactic Capacity	Lactic Power	Lactic Capacity			

Energy Systems – A Simplification

67

Table 3-2 Distribution of Energy Components Through Training and Competition

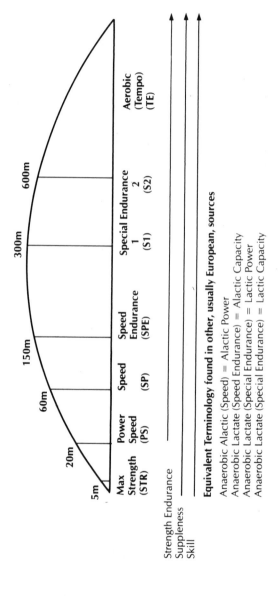

5m	20m	60m	150m	300m	600m	
Max Strength (STR)	Power Speed (PS)	Speed (SP)	Speed Endurance (SPE)	Special Endurance 1 (S1)	Special Endurance 2 (S2)	Aerobic (Tempo) (TE)

Strength Endurance
Suppleness
Skill

Equivalent Terminology found in other, usually European, sources

Anaerobic Alactic (Speed) = Alactic Power
Anaerobic Lactate (Speed Endurance) = Alactic Capacity
Anaerobic Lactate (Special Endurance) = Lactic Power
Anaerobic Lactate (Special Endurance) = Lactic Capacity

INTRODUCTION

Overview

It is not always easy in today's world of athletics to keep up with the new and rapid advance of knowledge.

Specialization has become the corner-stone for success. To succeed requires a thorough understanding of every detail of training – yearly periodization, macro and micro cycles, peaking, progressive loads and intensities. Coaches must have the ability to design sequenced work loads and intensities and know exactly what they wish to accomplish. Once done, intelligent adjustments can be made from a systematic examination of training sessions and feedback from individual athletes. It does not make sense to gamble. For some countries today's science has provided computers to do much of this programming, correcting and storing of successful systems.

High on the list of priorities to be understood are the energy systems and the training components which "challenge" each one. Fortunately, there is nothing mysterious about energy systems or about their effectiveness when they are thoroughly understood. It is the author's intention to provide the coach with a simplified and workable training system based on accurate scientific knowledge. For this reason, the presentation of each energy system is followed immediately by a discussion of the racing components which are fuelled by the system and the appropriate training which challenges the system to produce maximum output. At times, because of the lack of universal and accurate terminology related to energy systems between scientists and coaches, an attempt to bridge the gap will be made.

ATP - The Source of Muscular Energy

For a muscle to do work, it must contract (shorten) by sliding its actin and myosin filaments. This results in joint movement. A muscle contraction is a result of a complex chain reaction requiring energy. To change one form of energy into another, in this case chemical energy into mechanical work, is called transduction.

Energy needed for muscular activity is chemical energy contained in high energy phosphate compounds, notably adenosine triphosphate (ATP). ATP is the body's main source of energy for muscle contraction since it is held together with high energy phosphate (P) bonds. The reaction of ATP with water(a process known as "hydrolysis") results in a splitting of the phosphate group from the ATP providing an immediate source of muscular energy

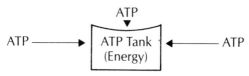

However, this ATP stored in the muscle is limited and could be depleted within 1 to 2 seconds unless recharged. To maintain muscular activity in the running muscles immediate production and replacement of ATP is necessary. It is useful to think in terms of an ATP "tank" that must be kept full or near full (never below 60% of its resting level) at all times for muscular activity to continue.

There are three systems or pathways available to refill this tank with ATP:

(1) anaerobic alactic
(2) anaerobic lactic
(3) aerobic.

ANAEROBIC ALACTIC ENERGY SYSTEM

The Role of Creatine Phosphate

An energy-rich compound in the muscle known as creatine phosphate (CP) provides an immediate source for the resynthesis of ATP. A transfer of a phosphate (P) from CP to ADP regenerates the necessary ATP from the ADP which remained after hydrolysis of ATP. Once again the ATP is broken down into ADP and energy. Under high

70

intensity exercise this process continues over and over until the CP stores are esssentially depleted. The enzyme responsible for the breakdown and transfer process of ATP resynthesis is creatine kinase (CK). This reaction is reversible.

$$ADP + CP \xrightarrow{\quad CK \quad} ATP + C$$

$$ATP \xrightarrow{\quad\quad} ADP + P + Energy$$

Resynthesis of ATP in this manner can only last for 4 to 5 seconds at maximum effort. Added to this are the initial 1 to 2 seconds of energy already available in the muscle, and approximately 7 seconds of ATP production is accounted for. This system is challenged as an athlete approaches top speed between 30 to 60 metres. It is therefore the system most closely linked with the component of SPEED (the third of the 5 S's). This high intensity, high speed work for short periods occurs without oxygen and without the build-up of the chemical products which begin to severely inhibit muscular action of longer duration. These products (commonly known as lactic acid) are actually made up of hydrogen ions and lactate. For these reasons, the system is known as the anaerobic (without oxygen) alactic (without lactate) system.

An Overview of Speed

It is questionable if training can significantly develop the capacity of the anaerobic alactic system. However, sprinting involves moving the body's limbs at the highest possible velocity and most certainly is related to the number of slow and fast twitch fibres found in the muscle. Alactic (speed) runs involve selective recruitment of motor unit pathways to improve the efficiency and firing of correct motor units. This in turn improves the development of force in the muscle. Within any muscle, hundreds of motor units are available to activate muscle contractions depending on the type, intensity and duration of the work called for. The whole process is not totally clear, but the complex recruitment and synchronized firing of motor units and muscles involves a motor learning process that must be rehearsed at high speeds to implant the correct patterns.

This speed component of anaerobic metabolism should be trained when no fatigue is present. International level athletes require 24 to 36 hours of rest or very low intensity work before doing maximum speed work. Sets of 3 to 4 repetitions with 2 to 3 minutes recovery between reps and 8 to 10 minutes recovery between sets is recommended for maximum results and to allow for the resynthesis of ATP and CP. The recovery rate for CP resynthesis is approximately: 30 seconds (50%), 1 minute (75%), 90 seconds (87%), 3 minutes (98%).

"Sprinting involves moving the body's limbs at the highest possible speed." Ben Johnson is the supreme exponent of this deceptively simple statement.

These figures demonstrate clearly the importance of 2 to 3 minutes between repetitions for recovery. No more than 4 sets, comprising 600 metres in total distance in a session should ever be done to challenge this system. A recommended session would be 450 to 500 metres, i.e. $4(30 + 40 + 50) = 480$ metres. Speed work (with technique) should be done to some degree all year round, although actual intensity will increase when a competitive effort is required.

"Sprinters are born, not made", is an axiom of many coaches. What about hurdlers? Does this axiom apply? Let's review a few facts about the sprint hurdle events:

HURDLING IS SPRINTING. Sprinting involves moving the body's limbs at the highest possible velocity or speed. The stimulation, excitation, and correct firing of the motor units makes it possible for high frequency movements to occur.

HURDLING IS A FAULTLESS SPRINT OVER BARRIERS. Hurdling speed is limited by one's technique. An athlete cannot run faster than his/her technique will allow. There is no room for error.

SPRINT HURDLING IS LEARNED THROUGH MOTOR EDUCABILITY. The skills of sprinting and hurdling must be learned at slow speeds first and then transferred to maximum speeds.

HURDLING CAN BE IMPROVED BY SPECIFIC TRAINING. A sprint hurdle race is comprised of a quick reaction time, acceleration, maximum speed and speed endurance (rhythm). To maximize the firing of the nervous system, NO fatigue can be present. After the hurdler's speed and rhythm over the hurdles has been established, NO 100 or 200 metre races are to be run before or during a major competition period. The two rhythms are different.

Speed Training

Speed is a product of stride length and stride frequency. Stride length can be improved by developing muscular strength, power, strength endurance and the proper skills of running and hurdling. The gifted hurdler with speed must channel and develop these other areas to reach his/her maximum potential. An average hurdler can become good. A good hurdler can become great. Stride frequency can be developed approximately 17% but for a very short

73

time by such methods as running with the wind, downhill (3%) running, and treadmill running, even towing behind a car. Speed and rhythm (speed endurance) are the keys to successful sprint hurdling. Guy Drut's fastest 100 metre is 10.4, yet with his effective rhythm, he was able to win his event (110 hurdles) in the 1976 Olympics.

Speed is defined as runs at 100% effort up to 60 metres or 6 seconds of effort with and without hurdles. Speed preparation involves an all-out controlled effort with no fatigue present.

Sample Methods of Speed Preparation

Without hurdles (with blocks or flying starts)
(1) "Step ups" 4 × 20m, 3 × 30m, 2 × 40m, 1 × 50m
(2) "Step downs" 1 × 60m, 2 × 50m, 3 × 40m, 2 × 30m
(3) "Pyramids" 1 × 60m, 1 × 50m, 1 × 40m, 1 × 50m, 1 × 60m
(4) Curves, straights using (i) to (iii)

With hurdles
Runs over 1 to 5 hurdles using similar methods as listed above with or without blocks. Any combination can be used up to 5 hurdles: 1 × 5H, 2 × 3H, 3 × 1H or 2 × 2H, 3 × 1H or 4 × 1H, 2 × 3H, 3 × 4H.

The "turnaround drills" illustrated below provide one form which such training could take. It is particularly efficient in use of space and thus lends itself to situations where facilities are limited.

Do not hurry speed preparation. Many times hurried speed training brings nothing but injury. If an athlete cannot continue at a satisfactory level - STOP.

Turnaround Drills

Single

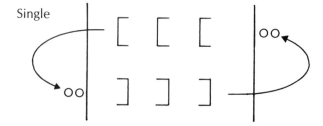

Team

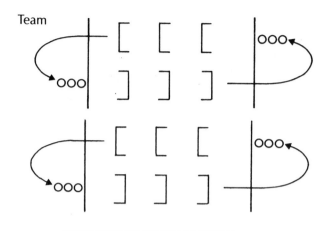

Motor Performance and Speed

The basis for the motor performance of sprinting and hurdling is the motor unit – consisting of the motor nerve cell in the spinal cord, the motor nerve fibre to the muscle, the end plate (between nerve fibre and muscle), and the muscle fibre itself. Radford[99] points out that a large number of motor nerve fibres serve each muscle and that the motor unit is "fired" at a rate, order and quantity determined by the motor task being performed. There are usually hundreds of muscle fibers per motor neuron. Centrally stored 'programmes' can fire thousands of motor units for the simplest tasks. He concludes that:

(1)   A good sprinter does not improve performance by firing bigger motor units but by synchronizing their firing to produce a greater rate of force development.

(2)   Sprinters have more fast twitch fibres (primarily in flexors) and their threshold for firing is extremely high; therefore under moderate work loads they are not used to generate force.

(3)   Sprinting involves a 'motor learning process', not just a physiological or biomechanical one.

It would appear possible to facilitate and establish relevant motor pathways. Since Radford[99] feels the limiting factors for controlling and moderating sprint performance lie outside the muscle itself, this motor educability leads us to consider the specificity of a final skilled and rehearsed pattern less likely to break down under stress.

Horizontal Speed = Stride Length × Stride Frequency

Stride length depends on two variables:

(1) Suppleness or flexibility in the lower limb complex; best obtained statically where all exercises are held for at least 15 seconds duration. Dynamic exercises then follow. However coaches must be aware of the possibility that optimal stride length varies for each athlete based on his/her limb segment lengths.

(2) Strength in the legs; impulse = force × time. In the hurdler's initial acceleration phase there is a relatively long time to develop and apply force to create maximum impulse. The angular velocity of the lower leg is slow in comparison to full speed running. Radford[99] points out:

   a) as speed increases, the time, force and impulse decrease, and the angular velocity increases
   b) when positive acceleration is over, the impulse is 0.

Acceleration will thus continue until the impulse is 0. This force-time relationship is where strength comes in, in terms of muscle type, and the type of strength preparation done. Stride frequency relates to the angular velocity of the legs. Again, as Radford[99] points out, this inherent quality can be perfected using specific motor learning skilled pathways.

From the discussion of the anaerobic alactic energy system and its duration, it can be seen that development in sprinting and hurdling speed is highly specific, and why many conventional training methods may give poor returns. Elements of speed must be practiced, rehearsed, perfected, under conditions of appropriate physiological stress. The question to be answered then is what type of work is required to get appropriate gains.

(1) Running speeds must be done using brief intervals with high angular velocity; this will ultimately bring into play the correct neuro-muscular pathways and related energy sources.

(2) Skill development must be pre-learned, rehearsed and perfected before it can be done at high speed levels.

(3) Flexibility must be developed, maintained and perfected.

Sequencing Speed

The sequencing of workouts is critical for a coach trying to maximize each single training session. For some time, the world's top coaches have used progressive loading techniques in the quest for world class performance. These techniques (often assisted by computerized tables) take into consideration variables such as total distance in a single or a series of runs, recovery times and percentage of maximum effort.

Even basic techniques have their value. Planning each day of the week for an entire year (every Monday, then every Tuesday and so on) enables each unit of preparation to be designed to produce a desired result while being easily sequenced to be more demanding than the previous.

Speed in workout patterns must allow time for the resynthesis of ATP & CP in the muscle. Sessions involving sets of 3 to 4 repetitions with 2 to 3 minutes recovery between reps and 8 to 10 minutes or "full recovery" between sets are recommended. NO more than 4 sets totalling 480 to 500 metres seems to be the upper limit in many European countries.

The following table (Table 3-3) illustrates 10 different sample distances or groups of distances used for speed workouts units. A series of 6 sequenced workouts is offered for each distance. The percent of maximum effort (95–100%)is adjusted in the table according to the time of year, purpose of session, weather conditions and chance of injury. Rest and recovery time will have a direct correlation with the times run. Each workout may be designated in sets: 3×30 or $2(3 \times 30)$. The latter notation is used to describe 2 sets of 3×30m. The total distance run in a session should always be stated.

In summary, it is by no means clear whether training does improve the production of energy through anaerobic alactic system. What is known is that the complex recruitment and firing of motor units is a motor learning process that must be rehearsed at high speeds to implant the correct pattern. The secret to speed simply lies in the central nervous system.

Table 3-3 – Sequenced Speed Workouts (without hurdles)

Workout	1		2		3		4		5		6	
Distance	*	+	*	+	*	+	*	+	*	+	*	+
30	3 × 30	90	4 × 30	120	5 × 30	150	2 (3 × 30)	180	2 (4 × 30)	240	2 (5 × 30)	300
40	3 × 40	120	4 × 40	160	5 × 40	200	2 (3 × 40)	240	2 (4 × 40)	320	2 (5 × 40)	400
50	3 × 50	150	4 × 50	200	5 × 50	250	2 (3 × 50)	300	2 (4 × 50)	400	2 (5 × 50)	500
60	3 × 60	180	4 × 60	240	5 × 60	300	2 (3 × 60)	360	2 (4 × 60)	480		
30–40	2 × 30 1 × 40	100	3 × 30 2 × 40	170	4 × 30 3 × 40	240	5 × 30 4 × 40	310	2 (3 × 30) 2 × 40	260	2 (4 × 30) 3 × 40	360
40–50	2 × 40 1 × 50	130	3 × 40 2 × 50	220	4 × 40 3 × 50	310	5 × 40 4 × 50	400	2 (3 × 40) 2 × 50	340	2 (4 × 40) 3 × 50	470
50–60	2 × 50 1 × 60	160	3 × 50 2 × 60	270	4 × 50 3 × 60	380	5 × 50 4 × 60	490	2 (3 × 50) 2 × 60	420		
20–30–40	2 (20, 30,40)	180	2 (20, 30) 3 × 40	220	2 × 20 3 (30, 40)	250	3 (20, 30,40)	270	3 (20, 30) 4 × 40	310	3 × 20 4 (30,40)	340
30–40–50	2 (30, 40,50)	240	2 (30, 40) 3 × 50	290	2 × 30 3 (40, 50)	330	3 (30, 40,50)	360	3 (30, 40) 4 × 50	410	3 × 30 4 (40, 50)	450
40–50–60	2 (40, 50, 60)	300	2 (40, 50) 3 × 60	360	2 × 40 3 (50, 60)	410	3 (40, 50, 60)	450	3 (40, 50) 4 × 50	470		

* – Suggested Workout   † – Total Distance Run

78

THE ANAEROBIC LACTIC ENERGY SYSTEM

The Process of Glycolysis

The demand for energy (ATP) dictates which energy system will be challenged, with the muscle adjusting to the energy system in operation at the time. After the seconds of activity under the anaerobic alactic system, the resynthesis of ATP and CP is no longer possible. Yet the ATP "tank" needs to be kept full if activity is to continue.

The next "gear" involves a process known as glycolysis. This is the breakdown of glucose (stored in the body in the form of glycogen) to produce energy. At the levels of intensity involved in sprinting and hurdling, this breakdown is done anaerobically with the resultant production of lactate and hydrogen ions (H^+) as waste products. The common notion of "lactic acid" being the waste product of glycolysis is not in fact true. It is the presence of the hydrogen ions which makes the blood acidic. This is thought to be a safety system which will eventually shut down the activity to prevent long term damage. For each lactate formed one corresponding H^+ ion is formed. This system operates in the sarcoplasm of the muscle and its chemical reaction is:

glucose + 2 P = 2 ADP —— 2 ATP + 2 lactate + 2 H$^+$

When glucose is used for this series of reactions, only 2 ATP are produced since 1 ATP is used to change glucose into glucose 6-P. When glycogen is used, 3 ATP are produced. Table 3-4 is a skeleton outline of the 11 anaerobic chemical reactions of glycolysis in the formation of pyruvate and lactate:

Table 3-4 Glycolysis

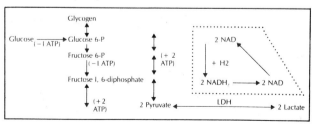

79

To summarize the equation: the breakdown of glucose or glycogen to pyruvate occurs anaerobically to provide high energy phosphates. This is made possible by the simultaneous reduction of the co-enzyme NAD which acts as a hydrogen acceptor (electron carrier). This reaction would soon stop if NAD (now actually $NADH_2$) were not regenerated. Here the formation of lactate comes into the picture. Pyruvate is reduced by the lactic dehydrogenase (LHD) system by accepting the hydrogen from $NADH_2$ to form lactate. The NAD can now capture and carry more hydrogen allowing more energy in the form of high energy phosphates to be provided for the transformation of ADP to ATP. Thus, the formation of lactate is not necessary for the delivery of energy, but it serves as a storehouse for the hydrogen, and thereby keeps the reaction going. Under anaerobic conditions the accumulation of H^+ ions is the limiting factor and is a major cause of fatigue in runs of 300 to 800 metres.

With fatigue, the built-in protective mechanism (the accumulation of lactate) will inhibit this system after 40–50 seconds of maximum effort. Although all energy systems basically "turn on" at the same time, progessive recruitment of each system occurs when one system is "challenged" more heavily because of the depletion of another. Only by challenging the right energy system will the desired physiological change and improved perfomance occur. Indeed at times, less work gives greater rewards since different tissues in the body react at different rates.

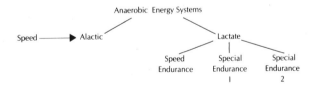

Most European countries use up to 300 metre runs to do high lactate work while the Italians are the exception, using distances up to 500m. To do this type of work requires rest, loose leg muscles, total relaxation and concentration. Without these conditions, the great possibility of severe injury exists. With the very high quality work involved in the lactate system, in most cases only 1–5 repetitions with full recovery can be done twice a week.

High quality lactate work can shock the body and the central nervous system. For this reason, loads (total distances or volume) and intensities (% of maximum) must be progressively sequenced in the same way as has been discussed in connection with speed training.

Recovery sessions are also sequenced in a set pattern. The number of years of the athlete's involvement in the sport (i.e. year 1, 2, 3 ... 10) plays an important role in determining the load and intensity in each unit. The load and intensity are increased separately to prevent injuries and to assist the health of the athlete. A year 3 athlete would not operate at the same level as a year 6 athlete and vice versa.

Within this lactic energy system, three components of competition and training can be identified.

(1) Speed Endurance (60–150m)
(2) Special Endurance l (150–300m)
(3) Special Endurance 2 (300–600m approx.)

The ability to maintain activity under increasing fatigue is known as stamina (the fourth of the 5 S's). As will be seen, stamina must be discussed in a wide range of physiological contexts.

Speed Endurance

Overview

To challenge this system runs are done at 95–100% or 90–95% intensity for approximately 7 to 20 seconds (60–150m). Under Gerard Mach's commonly used system and terminology, this is further broken down in Canada into Speed 2 (60–100m) and the first 50m of Special Endurance 1 (which extends from 100 to 300m). Like speed, this seems to involve a motor educability process to implant the correct patterns, and the improvement in the actual energy source. Speed Endurance runs can be done without the inhibiting disadvantage of a large lactate build up. Nevertheless, no more than 2 to 3 sets of 2 to 5 reps with 2 to 5 minutes recovery between reps and 8 to 10 minutes between sets are recommended.

Speed Endurance in the 100/110m Hurdle Events: The Concept of Rhythm

Many Eastern European countries place RHYTHM ahead of sheer speed, to the extent that rhythm may be called "hurdle endurance". Calvesi (Italy), Radiuk (Poland), Drut (France) and Sadovski (Soviet Union) have been showing the world for some time that there is more to hurdling than just running fast.

It is important at this stage to consider rhythm and its relationship to stride frequency. Firstly, it is known that athletes cannot run faster than their technique allows them. The skills involved in hurdling and sprinting must be learned until perfect. Repetition of mistakes means perfection of errors. Secondly, stride length can be improved by developing running technique, hurdling technique, muscular strength and muscular endurance. The result is to improve the neuromuscular mechanisms needed to coordinate the entire intrinsic loading and firing of muscles. Thirdly, the second variable of speed, stride frequency, can only be improved approximately 17% and for only short periods of time. The finite number of hurdles (10) and the finite number of strides between each (3) make the frequency even more critical. Hurdlers of widely differing abilities will all take 8 strides to the first hurdle, 3 strides between hurdles and 6 strides to the tape, but in times varying from 13.0 to 30.0 seconds! The relationship between rhythm and stride frequency becomes clear.

The following statements about rhythm from athletes and coaches show its important implications. "Rhythm is the speed which allows hurdlers to use their technique to the maximum." "Rhythm work increases the speed of the run." "I put the hurdles low so I can practice without tiring and be sure my hurdle technique is smooth. I can stay in rhythm and not lose pace between the hurdles". Simply put, rhythm is **"the running part between hurdles."** When training with the hurdles lower than racing height, hurdle technique becomes of secondary emphasis. Hurdling is a faultless sprint so we assume few technical errors exist for those doing the quality work of rhythm.

In high level hurdle races the hurdles "come up" closer as the race progresses. This same feeling can be rehearsed by moving the hurdles closer together. Rhythm is practiced by running over lower hurdles or hurdles placed closer together than normal, or both. Good technique must be maintained for the training to be effective.

The suggestions in Table 3-5 are specifically designed for the women's 100m hurdles, but simple alterations would make them applicable to the men's 110m hurdles. Specifications for drills may be altered to suit individual athletes' levels and phase of training.

Table 3-5 Rhythm Drills

1. 4 to 6 hurdles placed 7.8 to 8.0m apart at 76cm (30"); 13m to the 1st hurdle; standing or crouch start. Drill: 8 strides to the 1st hurdle and 3 strides between hurdles. Once mastered, move the hurdles 8.0 to 8.3m apart.
2. Same drill and specifications as in (1) with the distance to the 1st hurdle 21m for a 12 stride approach.
3. Same drill and specifications as in (1) with the hurdles laid flat on the track at a height of 40 to 65cm.
4. 4 to 10 hurdles 7m apart at 76cm (30"); 12m to the 1st hurdle with 3 strides between each hurdle using the lead leg or trail leg on the side of the hurdle only.
5. Hurdles placed 8.4m apart at 76cm (30") and 13m to the 1st hurdle. Drill: 8 strides to the 1st hurdle with 3 strides between for 5-8-10-10-8 hurdles. Full recovery between each repetition.
6. 4 to 10 hurdles placed 11.8 to 12.0m apart at 76cm and 13m to the 1st hurdle; standing or crouch start. Drill: 8 strides to the 1st hurdle and 5 strides between hurdles. Alterations as in (2) and (3) are possible.
7. Combinations of 3 and 5 stride pattern as follows: 13m to 1st hurdle, 8.4m to 2nd hurdle (3 strides), 11.8-12.0m to 3rd hurdle (5 strides), 8.4m to 4th hurdle (3 strides), 11.8-12.0m to 5th hurdle (5 strides) and so on to whatever number of hurdles is necessary.
8. All of the drills specified in (1) to (7) can be done with regular hurdle spacing but most have the lower hurdle height. Also any number of hurdle combinations from 4 to 12 hurdles can be used at regular or reduced spacings.
9. 6 to 10 hurdles, 13m to the 1st hurdle, 8.4m to the 2nd hurdle, 4m to the 3rd hurdle, 8.4m to the 4th hurdle, 4m to the 5th hurdle and so on to whatever number of hurdles are desired. Drill: 8 strides to the 1st hurdle, 3 strides between hurdle 1 and 2, 1 stride between 2nd and 3rd hurdle ....etc.

Many questions revolving around rhythm work have yet to be considered and answered. Is there any value in 7 stride rhythm between hurdles? Could rhythm work at

15 hurdles serve a purpose? The East Germans have a downhill ramp at a 3% grade for their sprinters to aid stride frequency. How about hurdles downhill at 3% grade? The Soviet Union uses "pulling machines" with harnesses attached to an athlete and a pulley on a roof to pull athletes at predetermined speeds to aid stride frequency. Could hurdle frequency be aided by such work? Why do the East German and Soviet athletes run 100m hurdle rhythm workouts the day before a major competition? As has been noted before, the Eastern European countries leave little to chance in racing and these methods deserve serious study.

Hurdle distances from startline

100m Hurdles

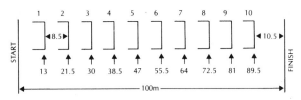

110m Hurdles

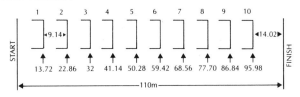

(3) Sequencing Rhythm

Speed Endurance runs challenge the anaerobic lactate energy system, the system that works strongest for approximately 7 to 40 seconds at high intensity. It appears that this system involves a highly specific synchronized motor pathway program which stores thousands of messages and signals to be implemented when called upon. In order to challenge this system specifically, workouts should be made up of no more than 2 or 3 sets of 2-5 repetitions. Recovery should be 5 minutes between reps. with a full recovery between sets. Table 3-6 offers some alternatives to specialized sequencing and race rehearsing. Again a series of 6 workouts is provided for sample training distances.

Table 3-6 – Sequenced Speed Endurance Workout   Without Hurdles

(*) Suggested Workout   (+) Total Distance run

Workout Distance	1 *	1 +	2 *	2 +	3 *	3 +	4 *	4 +	5 *	5 +	6 *	6 +
80	3 × 80	240	4 × 80	320	5 × 80	400	2 (3 × 80)	480	2 (4 × 80)	640	3 (3 × 80)	720
100	3 × 100	300	4 × 100	400	5 × 100	500	2 (3 × 100)	600	2 (4 × 100)	800	3 (3 × 100)	900
120	3 × 120	360	4 × 120	480	5 × 120	600	2 (3 × 120)	720	2 (4 × 120)	960	3 (3 × 120)	1080
150	3 × 150	450	4 × 150	600			2 (3 × 150)	900	2 (4 × 150)	1200		
80–100	2 (80) 1 (100)	260	3 (80) 2 (100)	440	4 (80) 3 (100)	620	2 (2 × 80) 2 × 100	520	3 (2 × 80) 2 × 100	680	4 (2 × 80) 2 × 100	840
100–120	2 (100) 1 (120)	320	3 (100) 2 (120)	540	4 (100) 3 (120)	760	2 (2 × 100) 2 × 120	640	3 (2 × 100) 2 × 120	840	4 (2 × 100) 2 × 120	1040
120–150	2 (120) 1 (150)	390	3 (120) 2 (150)	660	4 (120) 3 (150)	930	2 (2 × 120) 2 × 150	780	3 (2 × 120) 2 × 150	1020	2 × 120 2 × 150	

100m hurdles

With Hurdles (Rhythm)

Workout Distance	1 *	1 +	2 *	2 +	3 *	3 +	4 *	4 +	5 *	5 +	6 *	6 +
5H	3 × 5H	141	4 × 5H	188	5 × 5H	235	2 (3 × 5H)	282	2 (4 × 5H)	383	3 (3 × 5H)	423
6H	3 × 6H	166.5	4 × 6H	222	5 × 6H	277.5	2 (3 × 6H)	330	2 (4 × 6H)	444	3 (3 × 6H)	499.5
8H	3 × 8H	217.5	4 × 8H	290	5 × 8H	362.5	2 (3 × 8H)	435	2 (4 × 8H)	580		
10H	3 × 10H	268.5	4 × 10H	358	5 × 10H	447.5	2 (3 × 10H)	537				
12H	3 × 12H	319.5	4 × 12H	426	5 × 12H	532.5						

Touchdown Analysis – 100m and 110m Hurdles

Speed is the product of stride length and stride frequency, which in hurdling must take into consideration the time spent clearing the barriers. The fixed position of the hurdles determines to a very large extent the stride length as has been seen, with the resultant emphasis in stride frequency. Therefore, the position of the barriers can be used as a means to measure stride frequency, giving an indication of the extent to which flexibility and skill are reducing mechanical errors in the quest for the faultless sprint.

The time of the lead leg landing after a hurdle clearance is known as the "touchdown time". Touchdown times can be used to construct a realistic framework of an athlete's potential at different stages of his/her career.(Table 3-7) Specifically, since the length of the 100/110m hurdles races puts them within the limits of the Speed Endurance component, touchdown times in training are extremely useful in providing a constant read-out of the way training objectives are being met.

An analysis of some touchdown times from recent Olympic Games reveals that hurdle-to-hurdle TD times of 1.0 or 1.1 secs (0.9 secs in exceptional cases) can be reproduced nine times in a race, but only with a blend of perfect skill and preparation.(See Table 1-5)

Other premier hurdlers such as Guy Drut (France), Willie Davenport (USA), Johanna Schaller (GDR) and Grazyna Rabsztyn (Poland) have touchdown times of 2.4 to 2.5 secs at hurdle one and maintain a consistent 1.0 to 1.1 between hurdles. The touchdown charts shown here are based on these performances. Individuals with superior speed will be able to produce hurdle to hurdle times of 0.9 to 1.0 secs between hurdles 3 and 5 where maximum speed is reached. They can hold and reproduce times of 1.0 to 1.1 secs through hurdles 6 to 10. The 12 second barrier for women and the 13 second barrier for men will both be broken repeatedly in the coming years.

Table 3-7 – Touchdown Time (TD) Charts

Men - 110m Hurdles

Target	H-1	H-2	H-3	H-4	H-5	H-6	H-7	H-8	H-9	H-10	Finish
12.8	2.4	3.4	4.3	5.2	6.2	7.2	8.2	9.2	10.3	11.4	12.8
13.0	2.4	3.4	4.4	5.4	6.4	7.4	8.4	9.4	10.5	11.6	13.0
13.2	2.5	3.5	4.4	5.4	6.4	7.4	8.5	9.6	10.7	11.8	13.2
13.6	2.5	3.6	4.6	5.6	6.6	7.7	8.8	9.9	11.0	12.2	13.6
14.0	2.5	3.6	4.6	5.7	6.8	7.9	9.0	10.1	11.2	12.4	14.0
14.4	2.6	3.6	4.7	5.8	6.9	8.1	9.3	10.5	11.7	12.9	14.4
14.6	2.6	3.7	4.7	5.8	7.0	8.2	9.4	10.6	11.8	13.0	14.6
15.0	2.6	3.7	4.9	6.0	7.2	8.3	9.5	10.7	12.0	13.2	15.0
15.5	2.7	3.8	5.0	6.2	7.4	8.6	9.8	11.0	12.3	13.6	15.5
16.0	2.8	3.9	5.1	6.4	7.6	8.8	10.1	11.3	12.6	14.0	16.0

Women - 100m Hurdles

Target	H-1	H-2	H-3	H-4	H-5	H-6	H-7	H-8	H-9	H-10	Finish
11.8	2.2	3.2	4.1	5.0	5.9	6.9	7.9	8.9	9.9	10.9	11.8
12.0	2.3	3.3	4.2	5.1	6.0	7.0	8.0	9.0	10.0	11.1	12.0
12.3	2.3	3.3	4.2	5.1	6.1	7.1	8.1	9.1	10.2	11.3	12.3
12.8	2.4	3.4	4.4	5.4	6.4	7.4	8.4	9.5	10.6	11.7	12.8
13.2	2.4	3.4	4.4	5.5	6.6	7.7	8.8	9.9	11.0	12.1	13.2
13.8	2.5	3.5	4.6	5.7	6.8	7.9	9.1	10.2	11.4	12.6	13.8
14.0	2.5	3.5	4.6	5.7	6.9	8.1	9.3	10.4	11.6	12.8	14.0
14.3	2.5	3.6	4.7	5.9	7.1	8.3	9.5	10.7	11.9	13.1	14.3
14.8	2.6	3.6	4.9	6.0	7.2	8.4	9.6	10.9	12.2	13.5	14.8
15.0	2.6	3.8	4.9	6.1	7.3	8.5	9.7	11.0	12.3	13.6	15.0

Special Endurance 1

Special Endurance 1 is the component which comes into play when distances are extended beyond those dealt with in Speed Endurance. "Special" simply refers to the technical and the energy system demands. Runs are done at 95 to 100%(anaerobic) for approximately 20 to 40 seconds (150 to 300m) with complete or near complete recovery (10-20 minutes) between reps. 1 to 5 reps are done for this competition specific type endurance. The "1" distinguishes this component from Special Endurance 2, where similar demands are made under slightly different conditions (for 400m hurdle preparation only).

Special Endurance 1 has also been called "technique endurance" when talking about the 400m hurdles.

without Hurdles:

1. Runs over 150 to 300m at prescribed times and recoveries.
2. Ladder or pyramid workouts such as: 1 × 150, 1 × 200, 2 × 200, 2 × 250. Full recovery between sets.
3. Runs on curves and straights with and without blocks. Over 150–300m.

with Hurdles:

1. Runs over 3 to 8 hurdles (using touchdown times). 3 reps maximum. As hurdle 8 is 290m from the start, it is easy to calculate 300m's.
2. Runs of 6 to 8 hurdles working on the change down and the use of alternating legs and stride pattern adjustments.
3. Runs over 300m hurdles timing only the last 200.
4. Runs over 3 to 8 hurdles leading with the weak leg.
5. Runs over 8 hurdles with the last five hurdles lower or flat.
6. Runs over low hurdles for 150 to 300m.
7. Runs over 5 hurdles finishing with a run to 300m without hurdles. Record TD times.
8. Runs over 200m without hurdles then finish over 2 or 3 hurdles.
9. Run 3 hurdles, skip 2 hurdles, finish over 3 hurdles.
10. Ladder runs. 2 × 4H, 2 × 6H or 2 × 5H, 1 × 7H, 1 × 6H.

Table 3-8 400m Hurdles: A Race Planning Chart

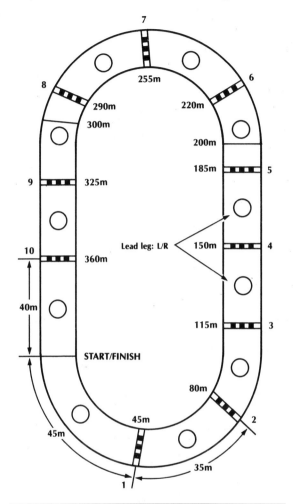

Stride Pattern	
Strides	Required Stride Length
12 Between	2.68m (8'9")
13 Hurdles	2.45m (8'0")
14	2.27m (7'6")
15	2.13m (7'0")
16	2.00m (6'6")
17	1.85m (6'1")
18	1.64m (5'5")

Special Endurance 2

Special Endurance 2 represents the upper limit of the anaerobic lactic system. As such it is appropriate only for 400 me tre hurdlers. 1 to 3 runs are done at 95 to 100% intensity for approximately 40 seconds to 2 minutes (300-600m) with complete or near complete recovery (20–30 minutes). Low intensity jogging or tempo runs (40–60% intensity) will help recovery and removal of lactate in 30 to 60 minutes. (If recovery is just walking or sitting, it may take 1 to 2 hours to remove the lactate accumulation). A common practice is to put the feet into the air or up against an object and shake them. This prevents the pooling of lactate-containing venous blood in the legs.

without Hurdles:

1. Runs over 300 to 600m at prescribed times and recovery.
2. Ladder or pyramid runs (400–500–400m).

with Hurdles:

1. Runs over 7 to 10 hurdles.
2. Runs over 5 hurdles for 200m and finishing the last 200m without hurdles or vice versa.
3. Runs over different combinations of hurdles as 1, 2, 3. 4, 8, and 9 while leaving out hurdles.
4. Runs over lower hurdles for 500m.
5. Runs 300m with hurdles then to finish.
6. Run 300m with no hurdles and finish with 3 hurdles.
7. "Unforgiving minute": run for 60 seconds as far around the track as possible with low hurdles.
8. Run 300m and then run over 5 to 8 hurdles with a 3 to 4 stride pattern.
9. Run over 4 to 8 hurdles at 100 or 110m hurdles distance and then progress to do a 200m or 300m.

Touchdown Analysis 400m Hurdles

As with the sprint hurdles, touchdown times in the 400m hurdles give a measure of rhythm and therefore a highly useful vehicle for monitoring training in the Special Endurance range. Edwin Moses has given us a look at the 400m hurdler of the decade. He displayed a remarkably

Table 3-9 – Touchdown Time (TD) Charts   Men - 400 Metre Hurdles

Target	H-1	H-2	H-3	H-4	H-5	200	H-6	H-7	H-8	H-9	H-10	Run In
46.2	5.8	9.4	13.0	16.7	20.4	22.1	24.2	28.2	32.4	36.7	41.1	5.1
46.6	5.8	9.5	13.2	16.9	20.6	22.3	24.4	28.4	32.6	37.0	41.4	5.2
47.0	5.8	9.5	13.2	17.0	20.8	22.5	24.7	28.7	32.9	37.3	41.8	5.2
48.0	5.9	9.7	13.5	17.4	21.3	23.0	25.3	29.5	33.8	38.2	42.7	5.3
49.0	6.0	9.9	13.8	17.7	21.7	23.5	25.8	30.1	34.5	39.1	43.6	5.4
50.0	6.0	10.0	14.0	18.1	22.2	24.0	26.4	30.8	35.3	39.9	44.5	5.5
51.0	6.1	10.2	14.3	18.5	22.7	24.5	27.0	31.4	35.9	40.6	45.9	5.6

Women - 400 Metre Hurdles

Target	H-1	H-2	H-3	H-4	H-5	200	H-6	H-7	H-8	H-9	H-10	Run In
52.0	6.1	10.3	14.5	18.8	23.1	25.0	27.5	32.0	36.7	41.4	46.3	5.7
54.0	6.3	10.7	15.1	19.6	24.1	26.5	28.7	33.4	38.2	43.2	48.2	5.8
56.0	6.5	11.1	15.7	20.3	25.0	27.0	29.8	34.7	39.7	44.9	50.1	5.9
58.0	6.7	11.5	16.3	21.1	25.9	28.0	30.8	35.9	41.1	46.2	51.8	6.2
60.0	6.9	11.9	16.9	21.9	26.9	29.5	32.0	37.2	42.5	47.9	53.4	6.6
62.0	7.1	12.3	17.5	22.6	27.8	30.0	33.1	38.4	43.9	49.5	55.2	6.8
64.0	7.3	12.6	17.9	23.3	28.7	31.0	34.2	39.8	45.4	51.1	57.0	7.0

easy 13 stride race pattern, and like the Olympic champions of Mexico and Munich he had a 200m differential of 2 secs or less (Hemery in Mexico 1.5 secs, Akii-Bua in Munich 1.8, Moses in Montreal 2.0). This also is a base for the 400m touchdown charts shown below. In the future it is likely that a 12–13 stride pattern will emerge among the leaders in this event.

The women's 400m hurdle world record will drop to the low 50's when women of great speed, flexibility and skill attempt this event. As for the men, a 2.0 to 3.0 secs difference between the 400m flat and 400m hurdle time should be possible for appropriately trained women. We will also see women using a 14–15 stride pattern.

THE AEROBIC ENERGY SYSTEM

The Role of Oxygen

The two systems of energy production described in previous sections are used to fuel activity of great intensity over a comparatively short duration.

If the activity is to continue for a long duration, the ATP "tank" in the muscle must be kept continuously refilled and the production of lactate and hydrogen ions must be avoided because they inhibit muscular action.

This is achieved using a system of energy production which uses an "ingredient" which has not previously been part of the chemical reactions, but which exists in great quantities – oxygen. The system using oxygen is known as the aerobic system. It is capable of fuelling low intensity muscular activity for enormous lengths of time – indeed it is continuous operation from birth to death, except when the need arises for intense activity in specific muscles.

In the aerobic system, pyruvate (from glycogen and glucose) and fatty acids (from stored fats) are first converted to acetyl CoA, which is then oxidized to carbon dioxide and water. Oxidation of acetyl CoA results from a complex chain of reactions known as the Krebs Cycle (citric acid cycle) and occurs in the electron transport system operating in the mitochondria of the muscle cell. The carbon atoms of acetyl CoA are converted to carbon dioxide and the hydrogens (containing electrons) are transferred to oxygen to form water. (Table 3-9)

This oxidization of glucose produces 36 ATP (37 ATP if glycogen is oxidized). This is clearly many times greater than in the anaerobic production of ATP.

$$Glycogen + P + ADP + O_2 \longrightarrow 37\ ATP + CO_2 + H_2O$$

Table 3-10 Aerobic Energy System

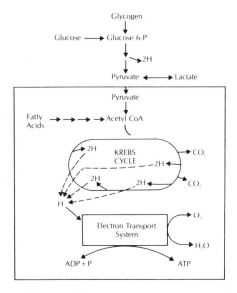

Note: If the aerobic energy system cannot supply enough O_2 the pyruvate must play the role of hydrogen acceptor and form lactate. This is the critical step in the whole process since the lactate will eventually shut down all the energy systems.

Training the Aerobic System

Hurdle events last for just over a minute at their longest, and are therefore anaerobic. Nevertheless a well developed aerobic system provides indirect, but significant support to hurdlers. As every distance coach knows, the aerobic system is highly trainable and the physiological changes which are produced as a result of aerobic training assist recovery and reduce the accumulation of fatigue from more specific hurdle training.

Moreover, it must be remembered that all energy systems are always available for operation instantaneously. A higher level of aerobic conditioning can therefore support higher levels of intensity and effectively postpone the point at which the muscular action becomes totally anaerobic, with the resulting production of inhibiting lactate.

Tempo Endurance

Aerobic training is therefore not to be neglected. The objective is to build a sound base on which specific quality work can be done. Aerobic training is commonly referred to as "Tempo" training. The term refers not only to the intensity of the running which is lower than in anaerobic components of running but also to the smoothness and control which are striven for even at quite high percentages of maximum effort.

Three kinds of Tempo training are identified (Table 3-10)

(l) continuous
(2) extensive
(3) intensive.

Tempo work follows a progression through all three levels of increasing intensity and lays the base for the anaerobic and Special Endurance sessions which follow.

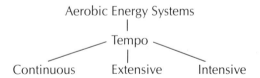

Continuous Tempo: (General Endurance)

The concentration of lactate in the blood starts to increase at low levels when workloads exceed 50 to 60% intensity, depending on the condition of the athlete. Easy continuous runs help to improve recovery and to lower athlete's fatigue levels. The cardiovascular and cardio-respiratory systems of a highly trained athlete in some respects will show physiological characteristics above the norm. For example, blood volume is larger in a trained athlete. In addition, the body's capability of oxygen absorption depends upon the size and strength of the heart, the extensive network of capillary blood vessels and above all, the quality and amount of blood. The most important part of the blood with respect to oxygen uptake is the red corpuscle and the iron-containing hemoglobin (Hb) which readily combines with O_2. Therefore, the more Hb, the more O_2 it will be able to carry from the heart and lungs to the working muscles. All these characteristics are improved with general endurance runs, defined as continuous runs at 40 to 60% intensity such as long slow distance runs. 400m hurdlers are more likely to use variations of this type of preparation than their sprint hurdle colleagues. David Hemery (1968 Olympic gold medallist in 400 metre hurdles) was the 4th man on the University of Boston's cross country team!

Workouts should be done with a minimum heart rate of 150 beats per minute for a minimum of 18 minutes.

Methods:

1. 25 to 30 minutes of steady state running.
2. 30 to 40 minutes of steady state running.
3. 30 to 50 minutes of fartlek work.
4. long intervals of 100m runs followed by a 200m jog for recovery.

Extensive Tempo:

When running at 60 to 80% intensity (of aerobic capacity) the trained athlete will experience lactate formation. Lactate at these submaximal levels forms in larger amounts when the oxidative system is insufficient to meet the demands of the muscle, namely at the point where a temporary state of oxygen shortage or "oxygen debt" is encountered. Continuous running at "extensive Tempo" levels assists in the removal of the lactate. Extensive Tempo is defined as relaxed and smooth repetition running at 60 to 80% intensity to assist recovery. Up to 20–30 reps can be done when the pulse rate is between 125–130. Extensive Tempo enhances the oxidative apparatus and lays a base for higher intensity work where lactate levels are higher.

Intensive Tempo: (Shared aerobic and anaerobic systems)

Intensive Tempo work borders on Speed Endurance and Special Endurance and therefore is an anaerobic/aerobic system. Lactate levels are quite high. Intensive Tempo, however, concentrates on the quantity and control of the running and the avoidance of undue stress.

To run at 80 to 90% + intensity a relaxed, smooth and controlled pace is required. Stress develops from running tightly with poor relaxation resulting in a type of emotional fatigue. The athlete may not necessarily get tired from running fast but from straining to work harder. Insufficient oxygen and the build up of lactate combine to bring muscle activity to a stop. The onset of this fatigue is determined to a large extent by the physiological changes begun as a result of continuous and extensive Tempo preparation and further developed with intensive Tempo. 6 to 12 reps can be done when a recovery pulse rate of 110–115 is reached. Runs may be up to 600m.

Table 3-11 Energy Systems Challenged by Tempo Endurance

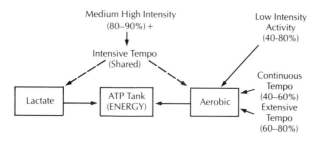

	Intensive Tempo	Extensive Tempo	Continuous Tempo
Intensity	80-90%	60-80%	40-60%
Distances	100-400	100-400	long
Reps	6-12	6-30	—

Intensive and Extensive Tempo Endurance Methods

The variables in repetition Tempo running can be expressed in the word D.I.R.T. "D" represents the distance to be run; "I" the interval; "R" the number of repetitions; "T" the time of repetitions and recovery.

The following workouts are creative ideas which use the variables to make interesting sessions for extensive and intensive Tempo training. The coach is limited only by the imagination and a knowledge of the basic principles.

Methods:

1. **"Paarlaufs":** continuous relays by teams of two or more athletes. Paarlaufs can be done on a track or in any suitable open area. A "rule of thumb" for the formation of teams is that there should be one more athlete per team than there are exchange points. One athlete is placed at each exchange, with two at the start/finish point. Legs can be of any desired length and need not be the same. Any number of repetitions can be run by each athlete; a common form of paarlauf is for the event to last a predetermined amount of time. Paarlaufs between closely matched teams are extremely competitive and enjoyable. One particularly demanding version is the "two-man" paarlauf on a track or similar area. If the legs are 200m long, each partner has to jog across the infield to the starting points after handing off the baton in order to receive it again from the other runner!

2. **"Fun days"** are workouts comprised mainly of relays. "Fun" must involve work. Any number of relay teams can be set up with each athlete running a set distance such as 4 × 200m, 4 × 400m, 400-300-300-200 relay. Again, the choice is unlimited. Points are awarded for placings: 1st – 3 points, 2nd –2 points and 3rd – 1 point. The first team to get 15 points wins the day. Competition, Tempo running and hard work blend together into a most enjoyable session.

3. **Ladders' or pyramids:** could include 1 × 200, 300, 400, 500 with a 100 walk between repetitions. Pushups and situps after each repetition.

4. **"Hurdlers' Fartlek"** 10 × 300 at varying intensities (60-80%) or (80-90%) on grass.

Hills

Each training system has its own form of creativity and necessary areas to bring out a little extra in each athlete. Running various distances, terrains and types of hills are nothing new to the track and field world. Long distance runners have long advocated hill running – a recommendation that has been taken to heart by sprinters and hurdlers. The use of hills has long been a cornerstone to our training system. The following ideas suggest modifications of hill work to tailor the energy system requirements to whatever the coach desires. Running hills can serve three purposes:

1. to develop anaerobic capacity
2. to develop aerobic capacity
3. to help create the competitive "animal" for racing situations.

The following workouts have proven very successful for developing ALL of the above goals. Choose carefully what you wish to accomplish. Hills can be run in sand, grass, snow, mud or gravel, even water in some places! The incline may vary from 3–5% to 25% at distances of 20 to 200 metres. Not all the workouts listed will suit all hurdlers but they may provide ideas for the use of hills which may be appropriate to each hurdler's development.

Methods:

1. **5-10-15 second drills:** are designed for power. Athletes line up at a starting line at the base of a hill. On a whistle they run for 5 seconds uphill and then return to the starting line. The recovery between repetitions is 15 seconds. This procedure is repeated for 10 to 15 seconds. This is an excellent warm-up.

2. **Downhill runs:** a 2 to 4% grade provides stride frequency work and Speed or Speed Endurance work. Distances can vary between 40m and 500m.

3. **Power Speed exercises** as specified in the skill section are very effective uphill or downhill.

4. **Continuous relays:** around, over or between hills are a good warm-up.

5. **Penalty hills:** involves athletes running 5 times a given hill in 30 seconds per repetition. For every hill not done in the given time they receive a penalty – perhaps two more hills. Realistic times and repetitions must be used. An excellent session for mental toughness.

6. **Follow the leader:** over and around hills can provide a warm-up or very demanding workout if one chooses.

7. **30-60-75 second runs:** athletes are challenged to see how far up a hill they can go or how many hills they can do in a given time. "World records" can be established for each hill.

8. **Games:** very exciting on hills. Soccer, pin ball or borden ball becomes very interesting when the goals are at the top of a hill!

9. **Tempo:** Consider many of the workouts described in the "Tempo" section. They can be done on hills-paarlaufs, fun days, ladders, pyramids or fartlek.

SUMMARY

After the preceding discussion on the energy systems, their "pipeline" into the ATP energy "tank" and the training which challenges each one, Table 3-1 can be expanded to a more complete form as Table 3-12.

In discovering which system is "challenged" at the right moment, a coach can identify and fit into place the pieces of this puzzle called "energy systems". Over time and with athletes willing to produce a supreme effort when required, the rewards of an intelligent and systematic application of principles will more than repay the investment of hard work.

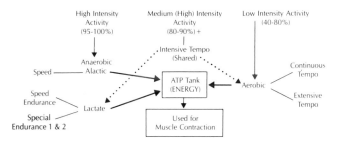

Table 3-12 Summary of Energy Systems and their Applications to Hurdling

Terms	Alactic	Anaerobic			Aerobic		
	Speed	Speed Endurance	Special Endurance I	Special Endurance II	Intensive Tempo	Extensive Tempo	Continuous Tempo
Intensity	95-100%	95-100%	95-100%	95-100%	80-90+%	60-80%	40-60%
Distance of Run	20-60m	60-150m	150-300m	300-600m	up to 600m	up to 600m	Long
Number of Reps/set	3-4	2-5	1-5	1-3	6-12	6-30	—
Number of sets	3-4(5)	2-3	—	—	1-3	2-3	—
Total Dist. in set	80-120m	150-600m	—	—	Long	Long	Long
Total Dist. in session	400-600m	300-1200m	300-1000m	600-1800m	600-4000m	Long	Very long
Recovery/Reps	1½-3'	2-5'	Near Full (10-20')	Full (20-30')	Pulse 110-115 (3-5')	Pulse 125-140 (2-3')	—
Recovery/Sets	8-10'	8-10'	—	—	Near Full (10-20')	Incomplete (5-10')	—
Examples Sprinting	1. 5 × 30 + 4 × 40 = 310m 2. 4(30 + 40 + 50) = 480m	1. 3(60, 80, 100) = 720m 2. 5(120) + 2 × 150 = 900m	1. 2 × 150, 2 × 200 = 700m 2. 3 × 250 = 750m	1. 3 × 400 = 1200m 2. 2 × 300 + 1 × 350 = 950m	1. 2 (8 × 100) = 1600m 2. 6 × 600 = 3600m	1. 20 × 200 = 4000m 2. 10-20 × 100 = 1000-2000m	1. 2-8km 2. Cross country runs
Hurdling	3. 5 × 50mH + 4 × 30mH = 370m	3. 3 (2 × 100H) = 600m	3. 3 × 200mH + 1 × 250H = 850m	3. 3 × 300mH = 900m	as above	as above	as above

Table 3-13 – Intensity Tables (From Haekkelob, Svenn Folkmann) Denmark

The charts give a guide to faciliate the selection of workouts at various levels of intensity for athletes of different abilities

TARGET TIME – 9.9-10.1   20.2-20.5   45.1-45.8

	100m	150m	200m	250m	300m	400m	500m	600m
95%	9.8- 9.9	14.9-15.1	20.3-20.5	26.1-26.5	32.6-33.1	46.6- 47.2	1:01.6-1:02.5	1:17.1-1:18.3
90%	10.3-10.5	15.8-16.0	21.4-21.7	27.6-28.0	34.4-34.9	49.1- 49.9	1:05.0-1:06.0	1:21.4-1:22.6
85%	10.9-11.1	16.7-16.9	22.6-22.9	29.2-29.6	36.4-37.0	52.0- 52.8	1:08.8-1:09.9	1:26.2-1:27.8
80%	11.6-11.8	17.8-18.0	24.0-24.4	31.0-31.5	38.7-39.3	55.3- 56.1	1:13.7-1:14.2	1:31.6-1:33.0
75%	12.4-12.6	18.9-19.2	25.7-26.0	33.1-33.6	41.3-41.9	59.0- 59.8	1:18.0-1:19.2	1:37.7-1:39.2
70%	13.3-13.5	20.3-20.6	27.5-27.9	35.5-35.9	44.3-44.9	1:03.2-1:04.3	1:23.6-1:24.8	1:44.6-1:46.3
65%	14.3-14.5	21.8-22.1	29.6-30.0	38.2-38.7	47.7-48.3	1:08.0-1:09.0	1:30.0-1:31.4	–
60%	15.5-15.7	23.7-24.0	32.1-32.5	41.4-41.9	51.6-52.4	–	–	–

TARGET TIME – 10.2-10.4   20.8-21.1   46.5-47.2

	100m	150m	200m	250m	300m	400m	500m	600m
95%	10.1-10.2	15.3-15.6	20.8-21.1	26.9-27.2	33.5-34.0	48.0- 48.7	1:03.5-1:04.5	1:19.5-1:20.8
90%	10.6-10.8	16.2-16.4	22.0-22.3	28.4-28.8	35.4-35.9	50.6- 51.4	1:07.0-1:08.1	1:23.9-1:25.3
85%	11.2-11.4	17.2-17.4	23.3-23.6	30.0-30.4	37.5-38.0	53.6- 54.4	1:10.9-1:12.1	1:28.9-1:30.3
80%	11.9-12.1	18.2-18.5	24.7-25.0	31.9-32.3	39.8-40.4	56.9- 57.8	1:15.4-1:16.6	1:34.4-1:36.0
75%	12.7-12.9	19.4-19.7	26.4-26.7	34.0-34.5	42.5-43.1	1:00.7-1:01.7	1:20.4-1:21.7	1:40.7-1:42.4
70%	13.6-13.8	20.8-21.1	28.2-28.6	36.5-37.0	45.5-46.2	1:05.1-1:06.1	1:26.1-1:27.5	1:47.9-1:49.7
65%	14.7-14.9	22.4-22.7	30.4-30.8	39.3-39.8	49.0-49.7	1:10.1-1:11.2	1:32.8-1:34.2	–
60%	15.9-16.1	24.3-24.6	32.9-33.4	42.5-43.1	53.1-53.9	–	–	–

TARGET TIME – 10.5-10.7   21.4-21.7   47.9-48.6

	100m	150m	200m	250m	300m	400m	500m	600m
95%	10.3-10.5	15.8-16.0	21.4-21.7	27.6-28.0	34.5-35.1	49.4- 50.2	1:05.5-1:08.6	1:22.1-1:23.5
90%	10.8-11.0	16.6-16.9	22.6-22.9	29.2-29.6	36.5-37.0	52.2- 53.0	1:09.1-1:10.3	1:26.7-1:28.1
85%	11.5-11.7	17.6-17.9	23.9-24.2	30.9-31.3	38.6-39.2	55.3- 56.1	1:13.2-1:14.4	1:31.8-1:33.3
80%	12.3-12.4	18.7-19.0	25.4-25.8	32.8-33.3	41.0-41.6	58.7- 59.6	1:17.8-1:19.0	1:37.5-1:39.1
75%	13.1-13.3	20.0-20.3	27.1-27.5	35.0-35.5	43.7-44.4	1:02.6-1:03.6	1:23.0-1:24.3	1:44.0-1:45.7
70%	14.0-14.2	21.4-21.7	29.0-29.4	37.5-38.1	46.9-47.6	1:07.1-1:08.1	1:28.9-1:30.3	1:51.5-1:53.3
65%	15.1-15.3	23.0-23.4	31.3-31.7	40.4-41.0	50.5-51.2	1:12.3-1:13.4	1:35.7-1:37.3	—
60%	16.3-16.6	25.0-25.3	33.9-34.4	43.8-44.4	54.7-55.5	1:18.3-1:19.5	—	—

TARGET TIME – 10.8-11.0   22.0-22.3   49.4-50.2

	100m	150m	200m	250m	300m	400m	500m	600m
95%	10.6-10.8	16.2-16.4	22.0-22.3	28.5-28.9	35.6-36.1	51.0- 51.8	1:07.7-1:08.8	1:24.9-1:28.3
90%	11.2-11.4	17.1-17.4	23.2-23.6	30.0-30.5	37.6-38.2	53.8- 54.7	1:11.4-1:12.6	1:29.6-1:31.1
85%	11.9-12.0	18.1-18.4	24.6-25.0	31.8-32.3	39.8-40.4	57.0- 57.9	1:15.6-1:16.9	1:34.9-1:36.5
80%	12.6-12.8	19.3-19.5	26.1-26.5	33.8-34.3	42.3-42.9	1:00.6-1:01.6	1:20.4-1:21.7	1:40.8-1:42.5
75%	13.4-13.6	20.5-20.8	27.9-28.3	36.0-36.8	45.1-45.3	1:04.6-1:05.7	1:25.7-1:27.1	1:47.5-1:49.4
70%	14.4-14.6	22.0-22.3	29.9-30.3	38.8-39.2	48.3-49.1	1:09.2-1:10.4	1:31.6-1:33.4	1:55.2-1:57.2
65%	15.5-15.7	23.7-24.0	32.2-32.6	41.6-42.2	52.0-52.8	1:14.6-1:15.8	1:38.9-1:40.6	—
60%	16.6-17.0	25.7-26.0	34.8-35.4	45.1-45.7	56.4-57.2	1:20.8-1:22.1	—	—

TARGET TIME – 11.3-11.4 23.0-23.3 51.0-52.8

	100m	150m	200m	250m	300m	400m	500m	600m
95%	11.1-11.2	16.9-17.2	23.0-23.4	29.8-30.3	37.3-37.9	53.5- 54.5	1:11.2-1:12.4	1:28.4-1:31.0
90%	11.7-11.9	17.8-18.1	24.3-24.7	31.4-31.9	39.4-40.0	56.6- 57.5	1:15.1-1:16.5	1:34.4-1:36.1
85%	12.4-12.6	18.9-19.2	25.7-26.1	33.3-33.8	41.7-42.4	59.9-1:00.9	1:19.6-1:21.0	1:39.9-1:41.7
80%	13.1-13.3	20.1-20.4	27.3-27.7	35.4-35.9	44.3-45.0	1:03.6-1:04.7	1:24.5-1:26.0	1:46.2-1:48.1
75%	14.0-14.2	21.5-21.8	29.1-29.6	37.7-38.3	47.3-48.0	1:07.9-1:09.0	1:30.2-1:31.8	1:53.3-1:55.3
70%	15.0-15.2	23.0-23.3	31.2-31.7	40.4-41.1	50.6-51.5	1:12.7-1:14.0	1:36.6-1:38.3	2:01.3-2:03.5
65%	16.2-16.4	24.8-25.1	33.6-34.1	43.5-44.2	54.5-55.4	1:18.3-1:19.6	1:44.0-1:45.9	–
60%	17.5-17.8	26.8-27.2	36.4-37.0	47.2-47.9	59.1-60.0	1:24.8-1:26.3	–	–

TARGET TIME – 12.0-12.3 24.5-25.3 55.6-57.7

	100m	150m	200m	250m	300m	400m	500m	600m
95%	11.8-12.1	18.0-18.6	24.5-25.3	31.8-32.9	39.8-41.3	57.4- 59.6	1:16.5-1:19.4	1:36.2-1:40.1
90%	12.4-12.8	19.0-19.6	25.9-26.7	33.5-34.7	42.1-43.6	1:00.6-1:02.9	1:20.7-1:23.9	1:41.6-1:45.6
85%	13.1-13.6	20.1-20.8	27.4-28.3	35.5-36.7	44.5-46.1	1:04.2-1:05.6	1:25.5-1:28.8	1:47.6-1:51.8
80%	14.0-14.4	21.4-22.1	29.1-30.1	37.7-39.0	47.3-49.0	1:06.2-1:10.7	1:30.8-1:34.3	1:54.3-1:58.8
75%	14.9-15.4	22.8-23.5	31.0-32.1	40.2-41.6	50.5-52.3	1:12.7-1:15.5	1:36.9-1:40.6	2:01.9-2:06.7
70%	15.9-16.5	24.4-25.2	33.2-34.3	43.1-44.6	54.1-58.0	1:17.9-1:20.9	1:43.8-1:47.8	2:10.6-2:15.8
65%	17.2-17.7	26.3-27.2	36.8-37.0	46.4-48.0	58.3-60.3	1:23.9-1:27.1	1:51.8-1:56.1	–
60%	18.8-19.2	28.5-29.4	38.8-40.1	50.3-52.0	63.1-65.3	1:30.9-1:34.3	–	–

CHAPTER 4

STRENGTH

... an athlete must not only be strong, but must be able to <u>use</u> this strength with speed."

Decathlete Daley Thompson demonstrates that great strength is not slow. He is a fine hurdler in his own right and a regular member of Britain's 4 × 100m relay team. In this photograph, the World and Olympic Champion is en route to his third straight Commonwealth Games Decathlon title, Edinburgh, 1986.

CHAPTER AT A GLANCE

INTRODUCTION

TYPES OF MUSCLE CONTRACTIONS

TYPES OF STRENGTH – A WORKING TERMINOLOGY
Strength Endurance
Power Speed
Maximum Strength

METHODS OF STRENGTH TRAINING
Basic Laws of Strength Training
Body Weight (intro, specificity, overload, reversibility)
Devices
Weighted Objects
Falling Body Weight (Special Strength)
Weight Training

INTRODUCTION

One of the major problems facing coaches as they research and attempt to interpret and use various forms of strength training, is the lack of common and accurate terminology. This chapter is intended to clarify the different ideas which may be encountered.

As with all components of training, coaches should approach strength training in the following general way.

(1) pinpoint fundamentals and accurate definitions of terms

(2) ensure the specificity of the training for the event especially with regards to the appropriate biomechanics and physiology

(3) devise methods for the development of components of strength.

TYPES OF MUSCLE CONTRACTIONS

The tension produced in a muscle can be of different forms.

Table 4-1 Types of Muscle Contractions

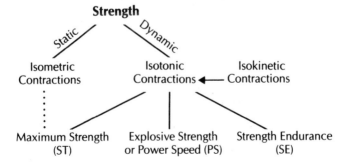

Isometric Static Contractions

During an isometric contraction, the length of the muscle remains the same. Both ends of the muscle are fixed and do not shorten to produce joint movement. Strength is being exerted isometrically when a person tries to move an immovable object. The weight does not move, but the muscles are producing great force.

Isotonic Dynamic Contractions

During an isotonic contraction, sufficient tension is produced to overcome a specific resistance so that it moves. The bench press, arm curls and jumping split squats are examples of isotonic contractions.

Isokinetic Contractions

Isokinetics are a type of isotonic contraction where the muscle shortens at a constant speed through its full range of motion. This is achieved by adjusting the resistance to the varying strength capabilities of the muscle at stages of the range. The "variable resistance" aspect of strength training is the feature of several new lines of exercise machines. Both isometric and isokinetic strength may play a role in the preparations necessary for track and field. Nevertheless most muscle contractions in hurdling are isotonic.

TYPES OF STRENGTH – A WORKING TERMINOLOGY

Strength is the ability of a muscle to exert force against a resistance. There are three basic kinds of strength produced by muscular contractions and strength work must be tailored to the strength gain required by the particular athlete. The types are

(1) Strength Endurance
(2) Power Speed
(3) Maximum Strength
See also Appendix A.

Strength Endurance or muscular endurance is the ability of a muscle to maintain its contractile force (tension) over a period of time (more than 10 seconds or more than 10 repetitions). It is achieved by loading 50 to 75% (or below – Mach recommends a maximum of 50% body weight) doing more than 10 repetitions with varied sets and recovery. There is no limit on the time or quantity except that which athletes require to maintain correct technique. Perfection of execution is required.

Strength Endurance (mixed) refers to doing a given exercise with body weight or with small added loads but not with weights or machines. These loads may be provided by weighted belts and jackets, sandbags or medicine balls and with resistances such as snow, sand, water, hills. Loads should be kept at less than 10% body weight. When performing skill exercises (A's, B's) always do more than 20m.

Exercises should be stopped if they are not performed in a technically sound manner.

Power Speed (or speed strength) is the maximum force a muscle can exert over a short period of time (less than 10 seconds or less than 10 repetitions). It is best developed by loading between 75% (or less – 50% body weight) and 90% of maximum and doing 6 to 8–10 reps. Execution of exercises must be quick but technically sound.

Power Speed (mixed) refers to doing a given exercise with added resistance (ie. sandbag, weight vest etc) but not with weights or a machine. Exercises do not exceed 10 seconds, 10 reps or 20m in distance. Perfection of technique is stressed.

The result of isotonic contractions of this type is quick joint movement – the speed which is so much a part of hurdling and sprinting. It is often referred to as "elastic strength" which implies the involvement of the contractile and elastic components of muscle. It is important to realize that an athlete must not only be strong, but must be able to use this strength with speed.

The same exercises can be done under Power Speed and Strength Endurance conditions as required.

Maximum Strength (or gross muscle strength) is closely related to isometric contraction, as it involves maximum muscle contraction at very low velocity. The higher the resistance the slower the contraction. It is best developed by loading between 90% (sub max) and 100% (max) doing a small number of reps and varied sets. No more than 20 sets – the total of all exercises – should ever be done in one session

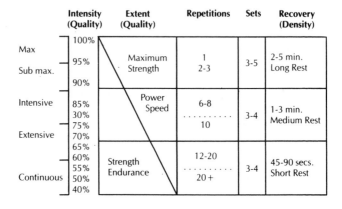

	Intensity (Quality)	Extent (Quality)	Repetitions	Sets	Recovery (Density)
Max	100%				
	95%	Maximum Strength	1 2-3	3-5	2-5 min. Long Rest
Sub max.	90%				
Intensive	85%	Power Speed	6-8		
	30%		. . . .	3-4	1-3 min. Medium Rest
	75%		10		
Extensive	70%				
	65%		12-20		
	60%	Strength Endurance	. . . .	3-4	45-90 secs. Short Rest
	55%		20+		
Continuous	50%				
	40%				

METHODS OF STRENGTH TRAINING

Basic Laws of Strength Training

Of the 5 S's, Strength is the one which perhaps most clearly reflects the basic laws of training:

SPECIFICITY: The load on a muscle must be specific to the fitness of the athletes and their event needs.

OVERLOAD: Gains in strength occur when muscles are progressively overloaded by one of the following methods:

(1) Quantity (extent): increases the number of repetitions
(2) Quality (intensity): increases the resistance or performs the repetitions faster
(3) Density: reduces the rest interval between sets

REVERSIBILITY: If specificity and overload in an athlete's programme decline, so will the athlete's strength.

In coaching, one accumulates a "mixed bag" of scientific knowledge and practical experience. The scientific knowledge allows a coach to identify the fundamental components of hurdling and to recognize weakness in specific fitness, flexibility, strength or skill within the framework of those components. But successful coaching involves more: the effective correction of these weaknesses may often require the creation of new exercises. The following pages describe methods of strength training by which problems specific to each athlete may be addressed and offer suggestions as to how those methods may best be used.

All strength programmes should be designed to prevent injuries while building strength. A system must be designed, based on the age of the athlete, individual strengths, weaknesses and needs, event specificity and the number of years he or she has been involved in sport. This information is blended with the basic laws of strength training listed above to design a series of general and event specific exercises.

Strength gains result from using a resistance in one of the following five methods:

(1) **body weight** as a resistance (push ups, sit ups)
(2) **devices** using a resistance to a specific movement (cables, accelerator, computerized harness)
(3) **weighted objects** while simulating specific skills (weight vest, sandbags, ankle weights, weighted shoes, medicine balls)
(4) using **falling body weight** as a resistance (depth jumping, hurdle hops, bounding). This type of training develops what is known as Special Strength
(5) **weights** as a resistance (Olympic weights, Nautilus, isokinetic resistance, Cybex).

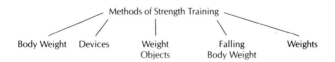

Methods of Strength Training

Body Weight   Devices   Weight Objects   Falling Body Weight   Weights

Body Weight

The weight of the athlete's body provides an effective and relatively safe resistance to muscle groups requiring development. Many traditional exercises exist (and others can be invented) which require little or no equipment to perform. The following section deals with the way in which these exercises can be put together into a successful strength programme based on modern principles.

Circuit and stage training provide such a basic, easily administered method. "Circuit training" refers to a series of exercises arranged and done in consecutive order. An athlete performs one set of an exercise and then moves on to the next exercise in the circuit. The entire circuit may be repeated several times.

"Stage training" uses the same underlying structure but ALL sets of an exercise are completed (with a recovery between sets) before the athlete moves on to the next set of exercises.

Complete *one* set of an exercise and then move on to a set of the next exercise.

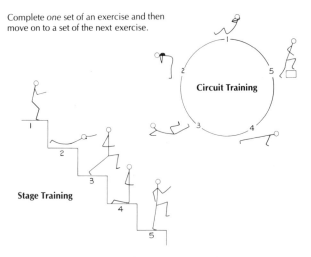

Circuit Training

Stage Training

Complete *ALL* sets of an exercise before moving on to the next exercise.

The following examples of circuits use only the athletes' body weight. They will be considered in terms of the laws of specificity, overload and reversibility and in the way they link Strength Endurance with the development of power.

Circuit "A" (Pillar)
Abdomen
sit ups (bent knee)
Back
good mornings
Abdomen
chinnies
Back
forward arches
Abdomen
jackknife (bent knees)
Back
chest raises

Circuit "B" (Ankle/Pillar)
Ankle
toe raises (in, out, straight)
Pillar
sit ups (feet up on box)
Ankle
ankle hops (low)
Pillar
twisting sit ups
Ankle
skipping (with rope)
Pillar
bicycle (feet in front)
Ankle
trippling (low ankle drives)

Circuit "C" (Legs/Pillar)
Legs
½ squats (arms in front)
Pillar
chinnies
Legs
running on the spot
Pillar
leg raises

Circuit "D" (Ankle/Arms)
Ankle
hop sideways (in circle)
Arms
clap push ups
Ankle
walk (hop) toe in and out
Arms
speed ball (punching bag)

Specificity

Each of the circuits listed has a specific purpose for a specific group of muscles. The endless choice of exercises for many different body parts can best be designed to meet individual needs ...to include ankles, feet, legs (adduction, abduction, flexion, extension), pillar (abdomen, back), arms (flexion, extension), total body exercises (complex). All circuits are designed to prevent injuries but can be used on alternate body parts if an injury occurs to one specific area. For example, if the hamstring is injured, work can continue on the ankles, pillar and arms while rehabilitation on the injured area occurs. The choice of exercises, number of exercises, specific muscle groupings and movement patterns required are left to each individual's needs based on strengths and weaknesses perceived by the coach.

Overload

Table 4-2 gives specifics to the meaning of quality, quantity and density. Regardless of the type of circuit, number of exercises or the specificity, the development of strength only comes with progressive overloading of a muscle group. The physiological adaptation to increased work loads basically allows the original load to become an "underload" as the enhancement of strength gain occurs.

Table 4-2 Specificity of Overloading

Number of exercises in a circuit	Work done in seconds	Recovery between exercises in seconds	Recovery between sets in minutes	Total time in minutes to do 2, 3, or 4 sets of a series of exercises		
				2 Sets	3 Sets	4 Sets
3	15	30	3	6½	10¼	16
4	15	30	3	8	13½	19
5	15	30	3	9½	15¾	22
6	15	30	3	11	18	25
7	15	30	3	12½	20¼	28
8	15	30	3	14	22½	31
9	15	30	3	15½	24¼	34
10	15	30	3	17	27	37
6	30	30	2	14	22	30
8	30	30	2	18	28	38
10	30	30	2	22	34	46
6	30	30	1	13	20	27
8	30	30	1	17	26	35
10	30	30	1	21	32	43
6	30	30	0	12	18	24
8	30	30	0	16	24	32
10	30	30	0	20	30	40
6	45	30	1	16	24½	33
8	45	30	1	21	32	43
10	45	30	1	26	39½	53
6	60	30	1	19	29	39
8	60	30	1	25	38	51
10	60	30	1	39	47	63
6	90	30	1	25	38	51
8	90	30	1	33	50	67
10	90	30	1	41	62	83
6	90	45	0	27	40½	54
8	90	45	0	36	54	72
10	90	45	0	45	67½	90
6	90	60	0	30	45	60
6	90	90	0	36	54	72
8	90	60	0	40	60	80

From this Table for example, it can be seen that to do 4 exercises at 15 seconds an exercise, with 30 seconds recovery between exercises and 3 minutes between sets would take:

2 sets........ 8 minutes
3 sets........13½ minutes
4 sets........19 minutes

With any variation of the number of exercises, work, recovery or sets, the principle of overload takes effect immediately.

Simply, the quantity can be increased by increasing the repetitions using time (15, 30 or 45 seconds) to do a specific number of exercises. Alternatively, the number of exercises can be increased by decreasing repetitions and doing them faster or by adding a resistance to a set number of exercises such as a weight vest or ankle weights. Density can be altered by increasing or decreasing the recovery between exercises or sets. This overload chart allows the coach to specify exactly how long a given workout will take once load and recovery are known. Such detail is not out of place in an effective programme. In the GDR there are specialists who are totally responsible for designing circuits for all sports to suit individual needs and events. Computerized programs have been used for some time with error detection and correction to prevent injury. Little is left to chance!

Power Speed may also be developed using circuit training when "Special Strength" (plyometrics, depth jumping activities) is introduced into circuits. Once a strong base of total body fitness (with specific emphasis on the lower leg and pillar) has been achieved, then circuits of 8 to 12 exercises which are introduced alternate an exercise for the body with one using Special Strength.

Repetitions may start at 4 and build to 10 but must be done fast and safely for all leg exercises. Body exercises may vary but will always be more than 10 (possibly 100's) reps. Exercises can be changed every 6 weeks but the sequencing of exercises and muscle groups stressed must remain the same.

Sample Power Speed Circuit
Body   chinnies
Legs hurdle   hops (double leg hops over 5 hurdles)
Body   clap push ups

Legs box jumps (.70m, 1 contact jump)
Body sit ups (knees bent)
Legs squat jumps etc. (10–12 exercises)

Reversibility

If an athlete expects gains in strength, then the principles of specificity and overloading must be adhered to, or the principle of reversibility will come into play and strength gains will drop off. Keeping records of progress and testing every 3 or 6 weeks are important to help set loads. Circuit training will also train many other critical components including coordination, balance, cardiovascular fitness, kinesthesis of event specific exercises and Central Nervous System patterns.

A Pillar of Strength

Specialized strength programmes are now paying attention to the fine details of preparation. The tremendous need for the centre of the body (abdomen, back) to be "a pillar of strength" has become more evident in the training of many of the world's top sprinters and hurdlers. By using circuit training with large numbers of repetitions many athletes from the GDR, Scotland, Italy and France have turned away from the conventional weight training systems which have been found to create injuries and tight muscles.

To allow the driving forces of the legs and arms to be smooth the centre of body strength must be strong since all force goes through the centre of the body. This type of strength is necessary to help running rhythm, relaxation and to maintain symmetry of motion about the entire body. Table 4-3 gives examples of exercises designed to create "a pillar of strength".

**Table 4-3 A Pillar of Strength
from Dr. Hervé Stephan (France)**

Abdomen

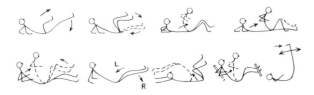

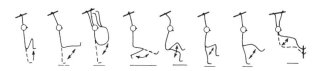

Bar

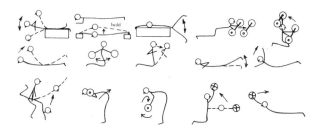

Back

Devices

Devices used in strength training may range from simple homemade ones which compensate for a lack of equipment in limited facilities to modern computerised technology. A knowledge of the muscles to be trained and the basic principles governing their training enables the creative coach to use a variety of devices.

Table 4-4 gives examples of many alternatives. Learning must come slowly and progress to faster speeds once perfected. An athlete must have flexibility and strength before working on speed. A weak athlete cannot progress forward. An injury will only result in delays. Once exercises are learned they are performed quickly in the starting movements and then taken slowly through the range of movement. The nervous system must be excited and fire the correct motor units related to the specific event needs.

Table 4-4 Exercises with Devices

Elasticated Cables

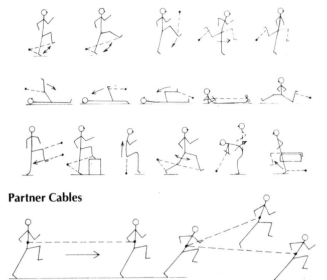

Partner Cables

Mechanical Devices

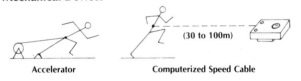

Accelerator   Computerized Speed Cable

(30 to 100m)

Weighted Objects

Teaching the body to feel certain positions, to perfect sprinting and hurdling skills, to implant motor responses, and to strengthen muscles requires carefully selected exercises designed to meet the needs, goals, phases and individuality of each athlete.

Performing the skills with the added resistance of a weighted object can assist the muscles of the body, both large and small, to coordinate and perfect the necessary movements.

Care should be taken that the weight is not so heavy as to distort or slow rather than to assist the desired action. (Table 4-5).

Table 4-5 Weighted Objects

Wrist Weights   Ankle Weights   Weight Vest   Weight Batons

Partner Drills   Partner Pull

uphill   Weight Vest   Sandbag
Downhill

Hurdle Uphill   Hurdle Downhill   Tire Pulling

Harness

Perhaps the most versatile and popular weighted object is the medicine ball. There are a large variety of exercises, of which Table 4-6 selects the most appropriate for hurdling.

Table 4-6 Medicine Ball Exercises

Flexibility

Strength
The Pillar (Abdomen Back)

Legs (Complex)

Table 4-7 Sample Medicine Ball Circuit

1. Warm-Up Drills: Circular movements around body. Passing with partner. General free/circular exercises.

2. Drop and Catch: Hold MB behind head. Drop and catch ball behind your back.

3. Continuous Chest Pass: Pass non-stop to partner. Vary height of throws and speed.

4. High-Low Pass: 6 to 8 feet apart. Squat and throw ball low to partner who is standing. Partner squats and throws ball back high.

5. Sitting Throw: Sit with legs flat in front. Vary the position of sitting (hurdler's sit variations). Keep ball in front of body when passing.

6. Volley Pass: Lie on back with partner standing above in straddle position. Partner drops ball while athlete on bottom catches ball (like volley) and returns ball like a bench press action.

7. Sitting-Rotation Pass: Sit with legs straight in front of body. Ball is passed from behind and caught on one side. Rotate and return on other side.

8. Sit up Pass: Catch ball. Rock back and pass to partner. Vary sitting and catching positions.

9. Squat Hop Passing: Squat position with short hop action. Pass to partner who is doing same action. Optional.

10. Back Lifts: Lay on stomach with feet and hands raised up. Pass ball to partner in same position.

Falling Body Weight

Special Strength ... Horizontal and Vertical

Without question Special Strength training (or plyometrics) now occupies a major place in the programmes of elite level hurdlers. Many studies have been translated principally from the USSR and GDR which support its physiological benefits. The research indicates that plyometric strength is "special" in that it bridges the gap between Maximum Strength and Power Speed (elastic, fast, explosive or ballistic strength). It is also closely linked with the physiology of the type of muscle fibre, speed of contraction, metabolic characteristics of the muscle, neuromuscular firing and the transfer of kinetic energy.

Plyometrics is a type of training in which a muscle is pre-stretched, forcing a rebound action commonly known as the stretch reflex (or myotonic reflex). It is now generally agreed that the kinetic energy from a falling body is absorbed by the contracting muscles in the amortization phase while the muscles are being forcibly stretched and is re-used in an immediate rebound phase resulting in a dynamic driving action. Simply stated, a concentric (shortening or overcoming resistance) contraction is much stronger if it immediately follows an eccentric (lengthening or yielding to resistance) contraction. Maximum neuromuscular tension is established in the least time. This training regime can be used for Power Speed (less than 20m or less than 10 repetitions) and for Strength Endurance (more than 10 repetitions or more than 20m of repetitions). Any skeletal muscle can be trained plyometrically, but the work applicable to hurdles involves the running muscles through jumping exercises and drills.

The following diagram will sets out the specifics of Special Strength (SS):

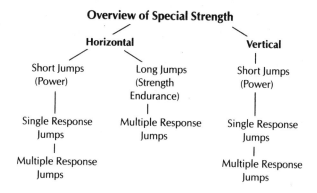

Special Strength has two distinct components: **horizontal** (jumps for distance) and **vertical** (jumps for height). Jumping exercises can further be divided into two types.

(i) **Short jumps** involve take-offs at full force and maximum effort under Power Speed conditions using single response jumps (SRJ) (a single take-off leaving the ground on one or both legs) or multiple response jumps (MRJ) (a series of sequential jumps either on one leg (such as hopping) or from leg to leg (such as bounding).

(ii) **Long jumps** involve take-offs at less than full force under Strength Endurance conditions using multiple response jumps (hopping, bounding, triple jump).

Physiologically, jumping exercises put a high demand on the tendons, muscles and neuromuscular system of the hip, knee and ankle joints. The learning and perfection of specific jumping skills must be technically correct and specific to the athlete's age, event, and physical and skill development. Restricted use of the exercises in young children from ages 10 to 16 is recommended since possible injury can occur to the spine and lower body joints. The load, recovery and exercise specificity (according to the basic laws of strength training) must be monitored to minimize the chance of injury. Single leg landings should be on the ball of the foot to avoid possible heel injuries. Take-offs should be explosive in nature upon ground impact with full extension at the hip, knee and ankle joints emphasizing balance and coordination. The knee joint must not collapse on landing or loss of force and injury may result.

Short Jumps:(Horizontal)

The overview (Table 4-8) outlines examples of jumps designed for horizontal Special Strength. "Short jumps" using single response jumps involve one jump for distance. Multiple response jumps involve mainly 3 to 6 foot contacts (jumps) for maximum distance. Many different jumps can be used, alone or in combination. Indeed, a "jumps decathlon"(Table 4-9) complete with points tables, has been a part of the training of jumpers for a number of years. Originating in Britain, its use has spread across the Atlantic and provides a simple and enjoyable method of testing short jumps (with the exception of the 25m hop which falls into the definition of a "long jump"). By using Power Speed through short jumps (SRJ and MRJ) an athlete's acceleration rate at the start may be improved. The method will also assist in developing stride length. Horizontal MRJ can be done from a standing position or with an approach run of 3 to 7 strides. They should always be done into sand or on soft matting to absorb the shock on the legs at impact. A maximum of 40 foot contacts per session is recommended. They usually are done before a sprint or hurdle session. It must be realized that Special Strength involves high stress work requiring a substantial strength base for the ankles, legs and back. Therefore (following the maxim that all training must be designed to prevent injury), initial loads must be moderate with lots of recovery. Increases must be gradual. For example, 2 sets of 8 bounds with 2 minutes recovery between sets can eventually work up to 5 sets of 8 bounds (40 contacts). The total contacts in a session using short jumps (Power Speed) should always be recorded.

Long Jumps:(Horizontal)

By using "horizontal" long jumps (MRJ), in Strength Endurance conditions Speed Endurance and Speed are developed. Research from the USSR recommends repetitions over 30 to 100m but more recently in Canada repetitions up to 150m have proven very successful for properly prepared athletes. Repetitions involving Strength Endurance are usually done after a training session has been completed. Besides the sessions listed in the overview, a variety of options can be introduced in sequences such as hops (right or left foot), hop + step, 2 hops + step, over 20 to 150m.

Distances of 30m, 50m, 100m and 150m can be used for testing by timing any of the series of jumps recommended. Data should be recorded and retests conducted at a later date. Likewise, the number of hops or bounds over the same distances should be recorded. The training should begin with moderate loads (20 to 40m) and build up to higher loads (50 to 80m) and beyond, if required. The chance of injury can be further reduced by observing a progression from bounding (using alternate legs) to the more stressful hopping on one leg.

Table 4-8 Overview of Horizontal Special Strength

Short Jumps (Power Speed)		Long Jumps (Strength Endurance)
Single Response Jumps	Multiple Response Jumps	Multiple Response Jumps
Session #1	Session #1	Session #1 (20-40m)
1. SLJ (ft. together) 2. SLJ (L ft. back) 3. SLJ (R ft. back)	1. 3 hops (L ft.) 2. 3 hops (R ft.) 3. 5 bounds	1. hopping (L ft.) 2. hopping (R ft.)
4. SLJ (turn to R) 5. SLJ (turn to L)	Session #2	Session #2 (20-40m)
6. Bwd. SLJ 7. SLJ (land L ft.) 8. SLJ (land R ft.) 9. Hop + SLJ (R ft.)	1. 5x (hop + step) 2. 2x (hop + hop + step) 3. 6 bounds	1. bounding
10. Hop + SLJ (L ft.)	Session #3	Session #3
	Jumps Decathlon (See Table 4-17)	1. 5 × 10 bounds 2. 5 × 20 bounds

SLJ: Standing Long Jump   R: Right   L: Left

Terminology
Hop: To jump, taking off and landing on the same foot.
Bound: To jump, taking off and landing on alternate feet in a sequence.

Short Jumps (Vertical):

Table 4-9 shows the available methods to apply SRJ and MRJ under Power Speed conditions which help to develop explosiveness, acceleration and speed. Work here is usually done at the start of practice and may consist of 4 to 6 jumping exercises with 6 to 8 repetitions. Usually a MRJ series will vary between 3 to 6 contacts but can reach 10 with high level athletes.

Opinions differ among experts about the height which can be used for the vertical component of jumps training and the landing technique. It is the author's opinion that vertical Special Strength should be developed following a strict progression. First the athlete should begin with straight leg ankle hops before moving to jumps over low objects (flat or low hurdles, boxes) where the height is in the area of 20 to 40cm. When jumping down from a height, it should also be 20 to 40cm with a straight leg landing and hands placed on the hips. The key to the exercise is the instant take-off with full ankle drive. Jumps then progress to MRJ over low objects and to jumps on the spot (knees to chest, vertical jump, using a single and double leg take-off). Finally, the athlete may advance to box heights of 50 to 90cm with a fall where 1 foot is slightly ahead or higher than the other at the start. The landing is on the ball of the foot with a bent knee to absorb the shock. Again, an instant take-off using an aggressive double arm action will follow. Jumps over hurdles or box jumps at 50 to 90cm heights may also be used. Once MRJ have been perfected using boxes and hurdles (includes depth jumps) combination jumps using a variety of combinations (as shown) are added. More recently this form of Special Strength has been appropriately called the "shock method".

The systematic control of exercises and sequencing from early to late phases must go from general to specific, from a few repetitions to many and from horizontal to vertical Special Strength. All the while, the design of the programme should be one which will prevent injury.

A variety of overload-resistance methods can be introduced after initial stages of development have progressed by using snow, sand, uphill, weight vests and sandbags as resistance. It is important to note that weighted resistance should be limited to 5 or 10% of an athlete's body weight with the total number of repetitions being cut by 50 to 60%

Training of this type is integrated in the programme in three week microcycles, followed by one week's rest, to capitalize on the body's bio-rhythms and rest cycles. Exercises may be changed every microcycle to accommodate individual athlete's needs. At least one easy day is needed between hard sessions. Special Strength should cease 8 to 14 days before a major competition. Special Strength should not replace other form of strength preparation but only be an additional means to improve.

Table 4-9 Overview of Vertical Special Strength

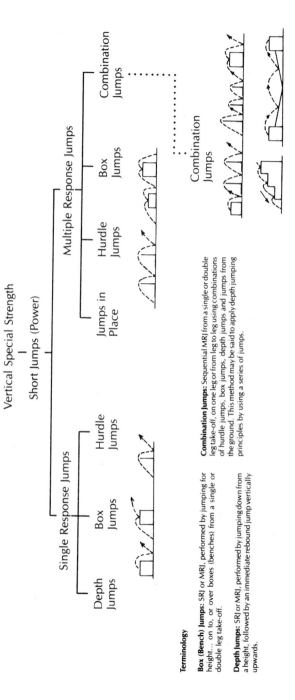

Terminology

Box (Bench) Jumps: SRJ or MRJ, performed by jumping for height... on to, or over boxes (benches) from a single or double leg take-off.

Depth Jumps: SRJ or MRJ, performed by jumping down from a height, followed by an immediate rebound jump vertically upwards.

Combination Jumps: Sequential MRJ from a single or double leg take-off, on one leg or from leg to leg using combinations of hurdle jumps, box jumps, depth jumps and jumps from the ground. This method may be said to apply depth jumping principles by using a series of jumps.

127

Weight Training

Traditional weight training has undergone significant development in recent years with considerable research into training effects, the introduction of new types of equipment and a much greater acceptance of the training in general.

Through all the changes, it remains one of the most effective methods of strength gain, virtually indispensible in the programme of a high level hurdler.

The following discussion assumes a basic knowledge of the exercises and their correct safe execution (Table 4-10). The concepts of macro- and microcycles and their relationship to programme planning is dealt with in greater detail in chapter 5.

Basic Cycles

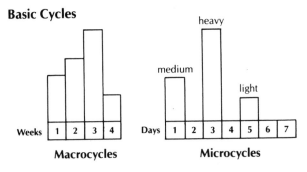

Macrocycles   Microcycles

Throughout the phases of a weight programme, training is arranged in blocks known as "macro cycles" which are designed to progressively build in volume for 3 weeks and then allow 1 week for recovery, thus giving a 3:1 ratio. (The 4th week may be used for testing or to develop some technical areas in hurdling). Each week forms a "microcycle" which is itself broken up into 3 sessions based on individual needs. Loading follows basically a medium, heavy and light sequence to provide a greater possibility for training stimulus. This microcycle of three sessions will gradually shift from general to specific, medium to higher intensity. Exercises may be grouped in pairs, working alternately the protagonist and antagonist muscles.

This shift in training emphasis results in "phases", divided according to different objectives.

Table 4-10 Sample Weight Exercises

Table 4-11 Overview of a Basic Weight Training System

	Sept	Oct	Nov	Dec	Jan	Feb	Mar	Apr	May	June	July	Aug
Phase	Preparation I		Competition I				REGENERATION	Preparation II		Competitive II		
Sub-phase	General Adaptation I		Specific Adaptation II		Pre-competition (Special Str.) III	Main-tenance IV	REGENERATION	General I	Specific II	Precompetition (Special Str.) III	Maintenance IV	
Strength	General Strength		Maximum Strength		Power Speed	Max Strength or Power Speed		General Strength	Maximum Strength	Power Speed	Maximum Strength or Power Speed	

REGENERATION

130

Phase 1: General Adaptation Phase

(4-12 weeks, 3 times per week)

This phase may also be called Build Up or Hypertrophy or Strength Endurance

Objectives:

1. To rehabilitate injuries and stabilize, protect and build joints.
2. To establish a warm-up pattern to prevent injuries.
3. To learn correct lifting techniques.
4. To work at medium intensity (60–75%) for 4 to 12 weeks to establish a Strength Endurance base (more than 10 repetitions).
5. To establish a testing procedure.
6. To develop muscle hypertrophy.

It will be during this phase that attention will be paid to developing the "pillar of strength" and the muscles of the ankles and feet by other strength training methods such as body weight programmes (circuit and stage training).

Table 4-12 Weight Training – Phase I

Generic Warm-up: 1–2 sets of 10–12 repetitions of each exercise at 50% load

	Session #1	Session #2	Session #3

	Bench Press
	Power Cleans
	Half Squats
	Hamstring Curls
	Sitting Press
	Good mornings
	  (light)
	Lunges (step forward)
	  (light)
		Half Squats
		Hamstring Curls
		Power Cleans
		Lunges (step forward)
		
		Pulldowns
		  (overhead)
		Reverse Leg Press + 1
		exercise of choice
			Front Squats
			Sitting Press
			Hamstring Curls
			Toe Raises

Week	**Session #1**	**Session #2**	**Session #3**
1	3 × 15 reps	4 × 15 reps	3 × 12 reps
2	4 × 15 reps	5 × 15 reps	4 × 12 reps
3	4 × 15 reps	5 × 15 reps	5 × 12 reps
4	3 × 15 reps	4 × 15 reps	Test

Phase II: Specific Adaptation Phase (4-8 weeks, 3 times per week)

This phase may also be called the Maximum Strength Phase.

Objectives:
1. To develop Maximum Strength (90% + intensity)
2. To lift correctly using selected rehearsed exercises in order to reduce the possibility of injury.

Table 4-13 Weight Training – Phase II

Generic Warm-up: 1-2 sets of 8-10 repetitions of 4 major exercises at 50% load, plus 2-3 exercises for the "pillar".

	Session #1	Session #2	Session #3
	Power Clean Hamstring (light weight) Half Squats Abdomen (light weight) Leg extensions	Pull snatch Abdomen (light weight) Full squats Hamstring (light weight) Reverse leg press 2 exercises of choice (light weight)	Repeat Session 1 or 2 or TEST
Week	**Session #1 (90% +)**	**Session #2 (90% +)**	**Session #3**
1	3 (5-6 reps)	2 (6, 4, 2 reps)	Repeat Session
2	3 (4-5 reps)	2 (5, 3, 2 reps)	1 or 2
3	3 (3-2 reps)	2 (3, 2, 2 reps)	or
4	2 (2-1 rep)	1 (2, 1 rep)	TEST

Phase III: Special Adaptation (Power Speed) (4-8 weeks, 3 times per week)
This phase may also be called the "speed strength" or "conversion" phase.

Objectives:
1. To establish a programme to develop Power Speed using less than 10 repetitions and intensities of 75–90% of maximum.
2. To continue testing procedure and improve results.

It will be during this Power Speed phase that it will be most appropriate to introduce Special Strength through methods such as falling body weight at medium intensity and low volume (40 contacts maximum) with the emphasis on correct technique.

Table 4-14 Weight Training – Phase III

Generic Warm-up: 1–2 sets of 8–10 repetitions of each exercise at 60% load

Session #1	Session #2	Session #3
Bench Press Power Cleans Half Squats Hamstring Curls Sitting Press Good Mornings (light) Lunges (step forward-light)	Half Squats Hamstring Curls Power Cleans Lunges (step forward-light) Overhead Pulldowns Reverse Leg Press One exercise of choice	Front Squats Sitting Press Hamstring Curls Toe Raises

Week	Session # 1	PATTERN ONE Session # 2	Session # 3
1	3 × 10 reps (75-85%)	4 × 10 reps (75-85%)	Special Strength
2	4 × 10 reps (75-85%)	5 × 10 reps (75-85%)	Special Strength
3	4 × 8 reps (75-85%)	5 × 10 reps (75-85%)	Special Strength
4	3 × 10 reps (75-85%)	4 × 10 reps (75-85%)	Special Strength

		PATTERN TWO	
1	1 × 10 reps (75%) 2 × 8 reps (80%)	2 × 8 reps (80%) 2 × 5 reps (90%)	Special Strength
2	2 × 8 reps (80%) 1 × 6 reps (85%)	3 × 8 reps (80%) 3 × 5 reps (85%)	Special Strength
3	2 × 6 reps (85%) 1 × 5 reps (90%)	3 × 6 reps (85%) 2 × 5 reps (90%)	Special Strength
4	Rest	Rest	
5	3 × 10 reps (75%)	2 × 8 reps (80%) 1 × 6 reps (85%)	Special Strength
6	3 × 8 reps (80%)	2 × 8 reps (80%) 3 × 5 reps (85%)	Special Strength
7	3 × 6 reps (85%)	1 × 8 reps (85%) 3 × 5 reps (90%)	Special Strength
8	Rest	Rest	Test

Phase IV: Maintenance
(4-12 weeks) (2 times/week)

Objectives:
1. To maintain Strength with minimal losses.
2. To maintain Strength components of training via weight (Power Speed, Maximum Strength).
3. To stay injury free.

Table 4-15 Weight Training – Phase IV

Generic Warm-up 1–2 sets of 8–10 repetitions of each exercise at 60% load
Exercises can be chosen from those done in Phase III. However, only 3–4 exercises would be chosen specific to the athletes' needs.

Maximum Strength Maintenance Sample

Week	Session # 1	Session # 2
1	3 × 6 reps (90%)	3 × 5 reps (90–95%)
2	2 × 6 reps (90%)	2 × 4 reps (90–95%)
3	1 × 6 reps (90%)	2 × 4 reps (90–95%)
4	1 × 5 reps (90%)	1 × 4 reps (90–95%)

Power Speed Maintenance Sample

	Session # 1 (50-70%)	Session # 2 (50-70%)
1	3 × 10 reps	2 × 10, 1 × 8 reps
2	3 × 10 reps	1 × 10, 2 × 8 reps
3	3 × 8 reps	2 × 8, 1 × 6 reps
4	3 × 6 reps	3 × 6 reps

Table 4-16 Loading Chart

MAX	70%	75%	80%	85%	90%
30	20	20	25	25	30
35	25	25	30	30	30
40	30	30	30	35	35
45	30	35	35	40	40
50	35	40	40	40	45
55	40	40	45	45	50
60	40	45	50	50	55
65	45	50	50	55	60
70	50	50	55	60	65
75	50	55	60	65	70
80	55	60	65	70	70
85	60	65	70	70	75
90	65	65	70	75	80
95	65	70	75	80	85
100	70	75	80	85	90
105	75	80	85	90	95
110	75	80	90	95	100
115	80	85	90	95	105
120	85	90	95	100	105
125	90	95	100	105	115
130	90	100	105	110	115

MAX	70%	75%	80%	85%	90%
135	95	100	110	115	120
140	100	105	110	120	125
150	105	115	120	130	135
160	110	120	130	135	145
170	120	130	135	145	155
180	125	135	145	155	160
190	135	145	150	160	170
200	140	150	160	170	180
210	145	155	170	180	190
220	155	165	175	185	200
230	160	170	185	195	205
240	170	180	190	200	215
250	175	190	200	210	225
255	180	190	200	215	230
260	180	195	210	220	235
265	185	200	210	225	240
270	190	200	215	230	245
275	195	205	220	235	250
280	195	210	225	240	250
285	200	210	230	240	255
290	205	215	230	245	260
295	205	220	235	245	265
300	210	225	240	255	270
305	210	225	240	260	275
310	215	230	245	265	280
315	220	235	250	270	285
320	225	240	255	270	290
325	225	245	250	275	290
330	230	250	265	280	295
335	230	250	265	285	300
340	240	255	270	290	305
345	240	260	275	295	310
350	245	265	280	300	315
360	250	270	290	310	325
370	260	275	295	315	335
375	260	280	300	320	340
380	265	285	305	325	340
385	270	285	305	325	345
390	275	290	310	330	350
395	275	295	315	335	355
400	280	300	320	340	360
410	285	310	325	350	370
420	295	320	335	355	380
430	300	320	345	355	385
440	310	330	350	375	395
450	315	335	360	380	405
460	320	345	370	390	415

MAX	70%	75%	80%	85%	90%
470	330	355	375	400	425
480	335	360	385	410	430
490	345	370	390	415	440
500	350	375	400	425	450
520	365	390	415	445	470
540	380	405	430	460	480
560	390	420	450	475	505
580	405	435	465	495	520
600	420	450	480	510	540
620	435	455	495	525	560
640	450	480	510	545	575
660	460	495	530	560	585
680	475	510	545	580	610
700	490	525	560	585	630
720	505	540	575	610	650
740	520	555	590	630	665
760	535	570	610	645	675
780	545	585	625	665	700
800	560	600	640	680	720

GUIDE

70% = 11–12 reps
80% = 7–10 reps
90% = 4– 6 reps
95% = 2– 3 reps
100% = 1 reps

Note (l) All % are rounded off to the nearest 5
(2) Units can be either pounds or kilograms

Table 4-17 Jumps Decathlon

	1 Standing Long Jump	2 Standing Triple Jump	3 2 Hops Step & Jump	4 4 Hops 2 Steps & Jump	5 5 Hops 2 Steps 2 Jumps	6 5 Springing Jumps	7 Standing 4 Hops & Jump	8 Running 4 Hops & Jump	9 25 Metre Hop (timed)	10 5 Stride Long Jump
100	3.73	10.51	13.00	15.54	19.15	17.06	17.67	23.77	2.07	7.28
99	—	10.43	12.90	15.46	18.99	16.91	17.52	23.62	—	—
98	3.65	10.36	12.80	15.39	18.84	16.76	17.37	23.46	2.08	—
97	—	10.28	12.69	15.31	18.69	16.61	17.22	23.31	—	7.26
96	3.58	10.21	12.59	15.08	18.54	16.45	17.06	23.16	3.00	—
95	—	10.13	12.49	15.01	18.38	16.40	16.96	23.01	—	—
94	3.50	10.05	12.39	14.88	18.23	16.25	16.86	22.85	3.01	7.23
93	—	9.98	12.29	14.78	18.08	16.15	16.76	22.70	—	—
92	3.42	9.90	12.19	14.68	17.93	16.00	16.61	22.55	3.02	7.21
91	—	9.82	12.09	14.57	17.77	15.84	16.45	22.35	—	—
90	3.35	9.75	11.98	14.47	17.62	15.79	16.35	21.99	3.03	—
89	—	9.68	11.88	14.37	17.47	15.64	16.25	21.79	—	—
88	3.27	9.60	11.78	14.27	17.32	15.54	16.15	21.64	3.04	7.18
87	—	9.52	11.68	14.17	17.17	15.39	16.00	21.48	—	—
86	3.20	9.44	11.58	14.07	17.10	15.23	15.84	21.33	3.05	—
85	—	9.37	11.48	13.96	16.91	15.18	15.74	21.18	—	7.16
84	3.12	9.29	11.37	13.86	16.76	15.03	15.64	21.03	3.06	—
83	—	9.22	11.27	13.76	16.66	14.93	15.54	20.80	3.07	7.13
82	3.04	9.14	11.17	13.66	16.50	14.83	15.44	20.65	3.08	—
81	—	9.06	11.07	13.56	16.35	14.68	15.34	20.42	3.09	7.11

Table 4-17 Jumps Decathlon

	1 Standing Long Jump	2 Standing Triple Jump	3 2 Hops Step & Jump	4 2 Hops 2 Steps & Jump	5 2 Hops 2 Steps 2 Jumps	6 5 Springing Jumps	7 Standing 4 Hops & Jump	8 Running 4 Hops & Jump	9 25 Metre Hop (timed)	10 5 Stride Long Jump
80	2.97	8.99	10.97	13.46	16.20	14.57	15.23	20.26	4.00	—
79	—	8.91	10.87	13.36	16.10	14.42	15.08	20.11	4.02	7.08
78	2.89	8.83	10.76	13.25	16.00	14.32	14.93	19.96	4.03	—
77	—	8.76	10.66	13.15	15.84	14.22	14.83	19.81	4.04	7.06
76	2.81	8.68	10.56	13.05	15.69	14.07	14.73	19.58	4.05	7.03
75	—	8.61	10.46	12.95	15.54	13.96	14.63	19.43	4.06	7.01
74	2.74	8.53	10.36	12.85	15.39	13.86	14.47	19.20	4.07	6.95
73	2.69	8.45	10.26	12.75	15.23	13.71	14.32	19.04	4.08	6.90
72	2.66	8.38	10.15	12.64	15.13	13.61	14.22	18.89	4.09	6.85
71	2.64	8.30	10.05	12.49	15.03	13.51	14.12	18.74	5.00	6.80
70	2.61	8.22	9.95	12.42	14.88	13.41	14.02	18.59	5.01	6.75
69	2.59	8.15	9.85	12.34	14.73	13.25	13.86	18.44	5.02	6.70
68	2.56	8.07	9.75	12.19	14.63	13.10	13.71	18.28	5.04	6.62
67	2.53	8.00	9.65	12.09	14.47	13.00	13.61	18.13	5.05	6.55
66	2.51	7.92	9.55	11.98	14.32	12.90	13.51	17.98	5.06	6.47
65	2.48	7.84	9.44	11.88	14.22	12.80	13.41	17.75	5.07	6.40
64	2.46	7.77	9.34	11.78	14.07	12.69	13.30	17.60	5.08	6.32
63	2.43	7.69	9.24	11.68	13.96	12.59	13.20	17.37	5.09	6.24
62	2.41	7.61	9.14	11.58	13.81	12.49	13.10	17.22	6.00	6.17
61	2.38	7.54	9.04	11.48	13.71	12.34	12.95	17.06	6.01	6.09

Table 4-17 Jumps Decathlon

	1 Standing Long Jump	2 Standing Triple Jump	3 2 Hops Step & Jump	4 2 Hops 2 Steps & Jump	5 2 Hops 2 Steps 2 Jumps	6 5 Springing Jumps	7 Standing 4 Hops & Jump	8 Running 4 Hops & Jump	9 25 Metre Hop (timed)	10 5 Stride Long Jump
60	2.36	7.46	8.94	11.37	13.56	12.19	12.80	16.91	6.02	6.01
59	2.33	7.39	8.83	11.27	13.41	12.03	12.64	16.76	6.03	5.94
58	2.31	7.31	8.73	11.17	13.25	11.88	12.49	16.53	6.05	5.86
57	2.28	7.23	8.63	11.07	13.10	11.78	12.39	16.38	6.06	5.79
56	2.26	7.16	8.53	10.97	12.95	11.68	12.29	16.15	6.07	5.71
55	2.23	7.08	8.45	10.87	12.80	11.58	12.19	16.00	6.08	5.63
54	2.20	7.01	8.38	10.76	12.64	11.48	12.09	15.84	6.09	5.56
53	2.18	6.93	8.30	10.66	12.49	11.37	11.98	15.69	7.00	5.48
52	2.15	6.85	8.22	10.56	12.34	11.27	11.58	15.54	7.01	5.41
51	2.13	6.78	8.15	10.46	12.19	11.17	11.42	15.39	7.02	5.33
50	2.10	6.70	8.07	10.36	12.03	11.07	11.27	15.23	7.03	5.25
49	2.08	6.62	8.00	10.26	11.88	10.97	11.17	15.08	7.04	5.18
48	2.05	6.55	7.92	10.15	11.73	10.87	11.07	14.93	—	5.13
47	2.03	6.47	7.84	10.05	11.58	10.76	10.97	14.78	7.05	5.07
46	2.00	6.40	7.77	9.95	11.42	10.66	10.82	14.63	—	5.02
45	1.98	6.32	7.69	9.85	11.27	10.56	10.66	14.47	7.07	4.97
44	1.95	6.24	7.61	9.75	11.17	10.46	10.51	14.32	—	4.92
43	1.93	6.17	7.54	9.65	11.07	10.36	10.36	14.17	7.08	4.87
42	1.90	6.09	7.46	9.55	10.97	10.26	10.21	14.02	—	4.82
41	1.87	6.01	7.39	9.44	10.87	10.15	10.05	13.86	7.09	4.77

Table 4-17 Jumps Decathlon-Record Sheet

	1 Standing Long Jump	2 Standing Triple Jump	3 2 Hops Step & Jump	4 2 Hops 2 Steps & Jump	5 2 Hops 2 Steps 2 Jumps	6 5 Springing Jumps	7 Standing 4 Hops & Jump	8 Running 4 Hops & Jump	9 25 Metre Hop (timed)	10 5 Stride Long Jump
40	1.85	5.94	7.31	9.34	10.76	10.05	9.90	13.71	—	4.72
39	1.82	5.86	7.23	9.24	10.66	9.95	9.75	13.56	8.00	4.67
38	1.80	5.79	7.16	9.14	10.56	9.85	9.60	13.41	—	4.62
37	1.77	5.71	7.08	9.04	10.46	9.75	9.44	13.25	8.01	4.57
36	1.75	5.63	7.01	8.94	10.36	9.65	9.34	13.10	—	4.52
35	1.72	5.56	6.93	8.83	10.26	9.55	9.24	12.95	8.02	4.47
34	1.70	5.48	6.85	8.73	10.15	9.44	9.14	12.80	—	4.41
33	1.67	5.41	6.78	8.63	10.05	9.34	9.04	12.64	8.03	4.36
32	1.65	5.33	6.70	8.53	9.95	9.24	8.94	12.49	—	4.31
31	1.62	5.25	6.62	8.43	9.85	9.14	8.83	12.34	8.04	4.26
30	1.60	5.18	6.55	8.33	9.75	9.04	8.73	12.19	—	4.21
29	1.57	5.10	6.47	8.22	9.65	8.94	8.63	12.03	8.05	4.16
28	1.54	5.02	6.40	8.12	9.55	8.83	8.53	11.88	—	4.11
27	1.52	4.95	6.32	8.02	9.44	8.73	8.43	11.73	8.06	4.06
26	1.49	4.87	6.24	7.92	9.34	8.63	8.33	11.58	—	4.01
25	1.47	4.80	6.17	7.82	9.24	8.53	8.22	11.42	8.07	3.96
24	1.44	4.72	6.09	7.72	9.14	8.43	8.12	11.27	—	3.91
23	1.42	4.64	5.99	7.61	9.04	8.33	8.02	11.12	—	3.86
22	1.39	4.57	5.89	7.51	8.94	8.22	7.92	10.97	8.09	3.80
21	1.37	4.49	5.79	7.41	8.83	8.12	7.82	10.82	—	3.75

Table 4-17 Jumps Decathlon

	1 Standing Long Jump	2 Standing Triple Jump	3 2 Hops Step & Jump	4 2 Hops 2 Steps & Jump	5 2 Hops 2 Steps 2 Jumps	6 5 Springing Jumps	7 Standing 4 Hops & Jump	8 Running 4 Hops & Jump	9 25 Metre Hop (timed)	10 5 Stride Long Jump
20	1.34	4.41	5.68	7.31	8.73	8.02	7.72	10.66	—	3.70
19	1.29	4.26	5.58	7.21	8.63	7.92	7.61	10.51	9.00	3.65
18	1.26	4.19	5.48	7.11	8.53	7.82	7.51	10.36	—	3.60
17	1.24	4.11	5.38	7.01	8.43	7.72	7.41	10.21	—	3.55
16	1.21	4.03	5.28	6.90	8.33	7.61	7.31	10.05	9.01	3.50
15	1.19	3.96	5.18	6.80	8.22	7.51	7.21	9.90	—	3.45
14	1.16	3.88	5.07	6.70	8.12	7.41	7.11	9.75	9.02	3.40
13	1.14	3.80	4.97	6.60	8.02	7.31	7.01	9.60	—	3.35
12	1.11	3.73	4.87	6.50	7.92	7.21	6.90	9.44	—	3.25
11	1.09	3.65	4.77	6.40	7.82	7.11	6.80	9.29	9.03	3.14
10	1.06	3.58	4.67	6.29	7.72	7.01	6.70	9.14	—	3.04
9	1.04	3.50	4.57	6.19	7.61	6.90	6.60	8.99	—	2.94
8	1.01	3.42	4.47	6.09	7.51	6.80	6.50	8.83	9.04	2.84
7	0.99	3.35	4.36	5.99	7.41	6.70	6.40	8.68	—	2.74
6	0.96	3.27	4.26	5.89	7.31	6.60	6.29	8.53	—	2.64
5	0.93	3.20	4.16	5.79	7.21	6.50	6.19	8.38	9.05	2.53
4	0.91	3.12	4.06	5.68	7.11	6.40	6.09	8.22	—	2.43
3	0.88	3.04	3.96	5.58	7.01	6.29	5.99	8.07	—	2.33
2	0.86	2.97	3.86	5.48	6.90	6.19	5.89	7.92	—	2.23
1	0.60	2.89	3.75	5.38	6.70	6.09	5.79	7.77	9.06	2.13

Table 4-18 Jumps Decathlon-Record Sheet

Trial No.	1 Standing Long Jump	2 Standing Triple Jump	3 2 Hops Step & Jump	4 2 Hops 2 Steps & Jump	5 2 Hops 2 Steps 2 Jumps	6 5 Springing Jumps	7 Standing 4 Hops & Jump	8 Running 4 Hops & Jump	9 25 Metre Hop (timed)	10 5 Stride Long Jump
1										
2										
3										

CHAPTER 5

PERIODIZATION

"Emphasis must be placed on the major objectives of the programme."

Mark McKoy (CAN) in the Olympic Trials, Winnipeg, 1984.

CHAPTER AT A GLANCE

THE PRINCIPLES OF PERIODIZATION

THE TERMINOLOGY OF PERIODIZATION
Periods and Phases
Macrocycles
Microcycles
Sessions and Units

SUPERCOMPENSATION

DESIGNING A PROGRAMME
Gathering Data
The Yearly Plan

SAMPLE PROGRAMMES

THE PRINCIPLES OF PERIODIZATION

Training objectives are important for incentive and to establish a training programme that is realistic for each athlete. Athletes should have at least two sets of objectives: (i) short range for a particular season; (ii) long range for a period of 2 to 4 years. The division of the training year to meet these objectives and to peak during a competitive period is called *periodization*. When there is one major competitive period over a 12 month period, this is called *single* periodization. If there are two major competitive periods (winter and summer) over a 12 month period, this is called *double* periodization. (See Table 5-1). Most modern hurdling programmes are designed on the basis of a double-periodized year and this is the model that will be discussed in this chapter.

The planning of training programmes has been in existence as long as there have been athletes and coaches. However, the scientific study of periodization began in the Soviet Union and became best known in the early sixties through the writings of L.P. Matveyev. Although many of his ideas have been refined and the methodology of programme planning has advanced tremendously, his basic concepts remain. The most easily accessible exponent of periodization theory in Canada is Tudor Bompa whose book *Theory and Methodology of Training* contains a comprehensive treatment of the subject. Frank Dick's *Sports Training Principles* also offers a focussed description of periodization designed to be used by active coaches.

To be successful, a training programme must be designed on a yearly basis at least. Success or failure may be based on the evaluation and identification of four areas of preparation: physical, tactical, technical and psychological. Once these have been established, the year's training can be divided into *periods*, namely preparation, competition and transition. These are then further divided into *phases*. Because of the cyclic pattern imposed by the phenomenon of supercompensation, phases are divided into *macrocycles* of 2 to 6 weeks in duration which are then divided into *microcycles* of 7 up to 10 days. Microcycles are further broken into training *sessions* each of

Table 5-1 Double Periodization (Matveyev model)

Month	Oct	Nov	Dec	Jan	Feb	Mar	Apr	May	June	July	Aug	Sept
Period	Preparation Period				Comp	T	Preparation Period			Competition Period		T
Phase	I		II		III		I	II		III	IV	V	VI

Performance ▬▬
Volume ▪▬▪▬
Intensity ••••••
T – Transition

100%

70%

Period	Preparation				Comp	T	Preparation			Competition		T
Phase	I		II		III		I	II		III	IV	V	VI

146

which is made up of *units*. Identification of training objectives of each of these areas must be matched by the knowledge of how to adjust and meet individual needs. The entire process of periodization is systematically designed for what is known as *peaking*. In the Terminology section, these terms will be dealt with in descending order of length. (See Table 5-2)

THE TERMINOLOGY OF PERIODIZATION

Periods and Phases

A *"period"* occupies a significant amount of time within the overall periodized year. There are usually three, encompassing the broad objectives of Preparation, Competition and Transition.

Within each period are various *"phases"* during which more specific objectives are set. The following outline illustrates the phases of a double periodized year. In this example, six well-defined phases can be identified.

- i) General Adaptation
- ii) Specific Adaptation
- iii) Complete Adaptation and Competition
- iv) Break
- v) Specific Competition
- vi) Transition, Recovery and Regeneration

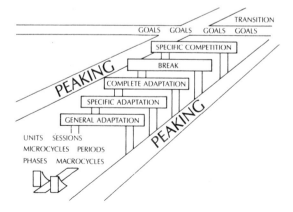

Phase I: General Adaptation (4-8 weeks)

Objectives: 1) To develop total body fitness by using sub-maximal training. 2) To identify, evaluate and test individual athlete's strengths and weaknesses to allow a programme to be designed to prevent injury.

This phase is like putting money into a bank in the form of reserves to build a base from many different components. A large number of different strength and suppleness exercises along with high volumes of extensive Tempo (60-80%) running and the introduction of speed work will give an athlete the necessary preparation base to enter Phase II. It is critical to complete this phase and not to hurry it, for specificity and peaking cannot occur without first establishing the body's total 'general adaptation'.

Phase II: Specific Adaptation (4-8 weeks)

Objectives: To progressively increase loads (volume and intensity), specifically for competition by event specific training.

This is the hardest phase demanding a gradual increase in volume followed by intensity increments. It may take 4 to 5 weeks to increase intensity by 10%, so movement here is slow. Each specific increase must match each athlete's capabilities to allow the body to adapt. If the athlete is unable to workout the next day after a session, then the workout was too hard and injury may result.

Phase III: Complete Adaptation and Competition (3-6 weeks)

Objectives: 1) To develop and maintain competitive performances to enable peaking by increasing intensity and decreasing volume. 2) To establish the correct number of competitions for peaking.

This phase of competition may be repeated both indoors and outdoors with specific objectives desired for each. Indoor competition may be used to evaluate and stabilize technique, to establish the correct number of competitions necessary to peak, and to achieve indoor personal bests by an expansion of competitive experiences. Outdoors this phase may be used to qualify for goals such as international team selection in which a true peak performance is necessary or to rehearse race patterns or rhythm which will last through the summer.

This phase represents the sum of all the work done up to this point. It is short and may consist of 7 or 10 day microcycles to allow the body to recover and to allow peaking. The more complex the technical demands of an event, the more competitions are necessary. The 100/110m hurdles will require 4 to 8 competitions while the 400m hurdles may need only 3 to 4 competitions before peaking.

This phase is the end of the first part of the yearly plan. From this point, a new preparation period would begin, building this time through to the main peak of the year — Phase V.

Phase IV: Break (2-4 weeks)

Objectives: 1) To provide a psychological and physiological recovery (regeneration), thus reducing the possibility of injury. 2) To make final adjustments in technique, race plans or peaking procedures. High level competition should be avoided.

Peaking should not be maintained very long at this point in time since it exhausts and strains the body. This phase introduces less intense work to stabilize major components for a final assault on the principal competition of the year, such as the Olympics or an international meet.

Phase V: Specific Competition (3-4 weeks)

Objectives: To produce optimal performance for the year.

This phase demands optimal intensity and REST. Rest is the single limiting factor to complete adaptation capacity. Little training occurs but is replaced with races and rest.

Phase VI: Transition

Recovery and Regeneration (3-5 weeks)
Objectives: 1) To recover psychologically and physiologically. 2) To recover using an active state while preventing major detraining effects.
3) To regenerate all training systems in preparation for the cycle to begin again in the new programme year.

Macrocycles

Macrocycles represent a division of a phase which varies between 2 to 6 weeks. As illustrated, macrocycles involve blocks or steps of loading using a specific ratio depending on the time and weeks that are available. It can be seen how increases in volume follow a "step" pattern, with a week of reduced load following the week of highest load to allow the body to recover and adapt. In the terminology of basic periodization theory, loading (volume or intensity) is usually expressed simply as high, medium or low. The example below shows possibilities of a macrocycle with a gradual increase in volume. Where loading is progressively built up over a period of time, the progression is known as *positive pulsation*.

Patterns of Macrocycles

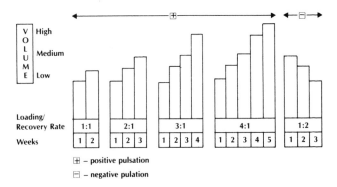

⊞ – positive pulsation

⊟ – negative pulation

A similar principle is used when the coach's intention is to reduce, not increase load. The final example above illustrates relative loads over a 3 week period building in recovery weeks for the specific needs of an athlete needing time to recover from previous heavy work. This type of loading pattern, where weeks progressively decrease in volume, is known as *negative pulsation*.

The variations in design of macrocycles gives the coach a choice of pattern depending on the desired result. There is no specific macrocycle pattern which will produce similar results for all athletes under all circumstances. They simply provide a framework and focus for coaches.

The relationship between volume and intensity in the design of a periodized programme can become quite complex depending on factors which affect the athlete. Simply put, however, high volume should be matched with low intensity. Conversely, intensity should be at maximal and submaximal levels only when volume is less.

The following illustration shows one method to maximize complete adaption by uniting intensity and volume. This cyclic structure of training allows for adequate recovery and regeneration of the internal body systems to prepare for increases in training loads.

Blocking (Steps) of Volume vs Intensity

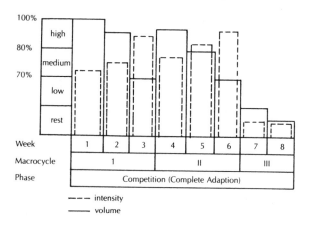

--- intensity
—— volume

Microcycles

Once the completion of the macrocycle patterns has been established, then the microcycle (7-14 days) must be set specifically for each athlete as suggested below:

Samples of Microcycles

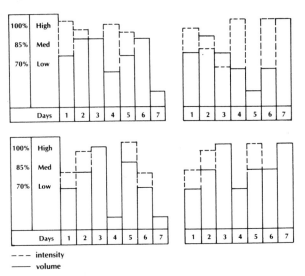

--- intensity
—— volume

Most hurdle coaches use a weekly microcycle of 7 days. No specific day of the week is used (i.e. Monday, Tuesday), but a number is given to each day (i.e. day 1, 2, 3) since the sequence of the days cannot be altered. Day one, for example, could start on any day of the week, depending on the last competition, recovery (often several days), injury or conflicting schedules in school or work. During competition phases a 10 day microcycle is often used to accommodate more recovery, travel to meets and higher intensities.

Table 5-2 Sessions and Units of a Sample Training Microcycle

UNITS / VOLUME	Day 1	Day 2	Day 3	Day 4	Day 5	Day 6	Day 7
	Warm-up Parts I, II	Continuous Warm-Up	Warm-Up Part I	Warm-Up Parts I, II	Continuous Warm-Up	Warm-Up Parts I, II	Regeneration
	Speed Endurance (Rhythm) (60-150m with hurdles)	Medicine Ball Drills	Games or Sport	Speed (20-60m with hurdles)	Medicine Ball Drills	Specific Race Corrections Speed or Special Endurance	
	Strength (circuits, weights)	Tempo (extensive, with recovery)		Strength Endurance ("A's" circuit, weights)			
	Tempo, with recovery			Tempo (extensive, with recovery)			
SESSIONS	Day 1	Day 2	Day 3	Day 4	Day 5	Day 6	Day 7

See Tables 5-14 to 5-20 for specific examples of microcycles suggested for the different phases of a programme.

Session and Units

The microcycle is further divided into *sessions*, or daily workouts, which may be single (one a day) or double (morning and evening) depending on the demands of the phase of preparation. Each session is further broken into training *units*, which each in itself have a specific goal, volume, intensity and degree of importance. Each session will have a unit which is the key purpose of the total workout with other units being of secondary importance. Table 5-2 shows a basic breakdown of a session into units. A warm-up unit is always necessary for Speed or Special Endurance to be maximized followed by Strength.

Table 5-3 Overview of Periodization Terms

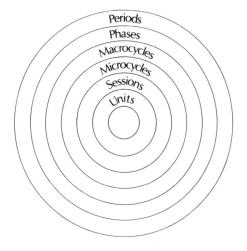

SUPERCOMPENSATION

The dynamics of adaptation will result only with the correct compromise between loading and recovery. Since loading follows the cyclic pattern of macrocycles, microcycles, training sessions and units, the process of adaptation can be examined. The concept of "supercompensation" is a key to understanding adaptation and tailoring training to capitalize on it. The letters which follow refer to Table 5-4.

Table 5-4 Supercompensation of a Training Session

a = from start to finish of loading; b + c = recovery from fatigue induced by loading to above original status; c + d = period of supercompensation a to d = period of time (0 = original status)

Training or loading (stimulus) which exceeds the minimum level (o) causes fatigue (a) resulting in a decrease in performance. During the rest period (b) the organism recovers (compensation) followed by a rebound (super-compensation) to a higher biological status (c) than the original level (o). If another stimulus (load) is not applied at the optimal time (during supercompensation), then the performance will return to its initial level (o). As an athlete adapts to the new stimulus, the load gradually increases as does the performance level. The progressive raising of loads in a cyclic pattern in turn raises an athlete's training status relative to a specific type of load and allows for complete adaptation (improved performance levels).

The principle of supercompensation not only applies to a single training session but also to a microcycle (7-14 day cycle), macrocycle (2-6 weeks), phases and even over a period of years. For this simple reason, loads are varied from day to day, week to week, and year to year. (See Table 5-5).

Table 5-5 Effects of Supercompensation

Microcycles and Supercompensation

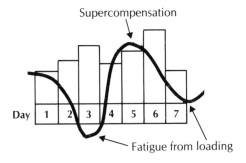

Macrocycles and Supercompensation

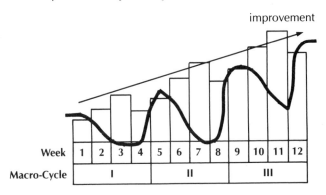

The systematic cyclic patterns shown above are designed to allow for both physical and psychological adaptation. There must be continuity between load and recovery as illustrated by macrocycle design which always accommodates a week of reduced loading after weeks of increased loading. If time for recovery is not properly accommodated, athletes become fatigued, which leads to injury or sickness or undue psychological stress. Furthermore, if adaptation does not follow the basic laws of overload with recovery built in (or, where athletes compete too much) the result is a state commonly known as 'staleness'.

For the elite athlete it may take 36 to 72 hours recovery between hard sessions to gain the effects of supercompensation. Further, increases in intensity can only follow a 5% increase every three weeks (10% every 5 to 6 weeks).

Conversely, new loads must challenge each athlete's present training status by being applied at the highest point of supercompensation. If training loads remain the same during supercompensations there will be a decrease in adaptation which may even result in a detraining effect. Improvement comes about very rapidly at the start of a new stimulus, but slows down when it approaches its limit of adaptation and will even decrease if a new stimulus is not applied at a higher level. The human body has a great capacity to adjust and respond to new training loads.

Continuity over years of training is necessary to succeed. Maximum development does require years of systematic design. Each year adds to the previous, and a long lay-off will bring about a detraining effect and a loss of forward progress which becomes more dramatic with age.

Supercompensation is training for adaptation. It does work and, when done correctly, facilitates the greatest single reason for athletic performance ... peak performances and personal bests.

Although the concept in general is a simple one, there are complications. These are brought about by psychological and external considerations which will always negatively effect an uninterrupted improvement. The coach will often feel in a process of "trial and errors", balancing the adjustments which need to be made with the general principles.

Table 5-6 Review of Training Terms: The 5 S's

SUPPLENESS or flexibility: is the range of movement at a joint
(a) PNF: exercises involve using a partner to provide a resistance
(b) STATIC: involves holding an exercise for 15 seconds or longer
(c) DYNAMIC: involves repeated movements through a range of motion

STRENGTH: is the ability of a muscle to exert force against a resistance
1) ISOMETRIC contractions: occur when insufficient tension is produced to move a resistance. No joint movement occurs.
2) ISOTONIC contractions: occur when sufficient tension is produced within a muscle group to overcome a resistance. Joint movement occurs.
(i) **Strength Endurance**: is the ability of a muscle to maintain its contractile force over a period of time (over 10 sec or 10 repetitions). Load 50-75% of maximum (or less) for 10-15 or more repetitions.
(ii) **Power Speed**: (fast, speed, elastic strength) is the maximum force a muscle can exert over a short period of time (less than 10 reps or sec). Load 75-90% for 6-10 repetitions (or less than 10 secs or 20m.).
(iii) **Special Strength**: involves a component of power using jumping exercises such as depth jumping, boxes, hurdles, combined jumps. Special Strength is gained through "plyometrics", with the emphasis on the muscles' eccentric contraction.
(iv) **Maximum Strength**: involves optimal muscle strength at low velocity. Load 90-100% of maximum for 1-4 repetitions (close to isometric contraction).

SPEED: is running at 95-100% maximum up to 60m or 6 sec (anaerobic alactic).

STAMINA or ENDURANCE: is divided into anaerobic and aerobic components
1) ANAEROBIC LACTACTIC (Energy System)
(i) Speed Endurance: is running at 95-100% of maximum (7-20 sec) over 60-150m. This is also classified as Speed 2 (60-100m) and Special Endurance 1 (100-150m) under the Mach system.
(ii) Special Endurance 1: is running at 95-100% of max (20-40 sec) over 150-300m. 1-4 Reps are done with full recovery between repetitions.
(iii) Special Endurance 2: is running at 95-100% of max (beyond 40 sec) from 300 to 600m. 1-3 reps are done with full recovery between repetitions.

2) AEROBIC: means the supply of oxygen meets the demand of the muscles. Tempo Endurance is a general term used to apply to aerobic runs.
   (i) Intensive Tempo: is running at 80-90% + of maximum up to 600m.
   (ii) Extensive Tempo: is running at 60-80% of maximum up to 600m.
   (iii) Continuous Tempo: is running at 40-60% of maximum over longer distances such as cross country runs or fartlek.

SKILL: involves teaching the body to feel certain positions through motor educability (kinesthesis). Basic skills must be done correctly under conditions of perfection. Doing skills wrong means perfection of errors. STOP doing exercises when done incorrectly.
1) WARM UP Part 1: a 2-3 lap jog followed by 3x3x50 (For 100/110m hurdlers) or 3x3x100 (for 400m hurdlers), after the first set, upper body flexibility exercises (dynamic), after the 2nd set, lower body flexibility exercises (static), after the 3rd set, skill exercises (dynamic). Part 2: 3-4x40m accelerations.
2) SPRINT AND HURDLE SKILL: A's, B's, C's (with and without hurdles)
3) STARTING SKILLS: falling starts, accelerations, techniques of start.

DESIGNING A PROGRAM

Gathering Data

With a knowledge of the principles and terminology of periodization and the components of a training system (the 5 S's, reviewed in Table 5-6), the coach begins to design a programme. This is based on each athlete's capabilities and an evaluation of the athlete's potential, priorities and objectives. This section deals with convenient ways to gather this data.

The athlete should provide a written record of his/her objectives. An index card can easily be adapted for the purpose and is readily kept on file by the coach. A sample is provided as Table 5-7.

The accurate recording and evaluation of results assists the coach and athlete to set realistic goals for the coming year. The form shown in Table 5-8 is one method to accomplish this. The athlete records all results and gives it to the coach at the end of each competitive season.

Table 5-7 Athlete's Objective Card

Name _____ Birthdate _____ CTFA# _____

Address _____ Phone# _____

Medical Ins. # _____ Height _____ Weight _____

Emergency Contact _____

Events (Order of Preference)	Best Performance	Date, Place	Goal for Year
_____	_____	_____	_____
_____	_____	_____	_____

Other goals in track and field _____

How do you see the role of your coach? _____

(Use reverse if necessary)

Table 5-8 Athlete's Yearly Results Sheet

Name Neville Douglas Age Class Junior OTFA # 5429 Year 1984

Event Specialty 400m Hurdles   Coach: Brent McFarlane

EVENTS   Phone _____

Date	Place or Event	Placing	400H	400	200	800	Comments: Previous pb's
May 10	Kitchener-Waterloo High School Champ.	1	55.1	49.3		2:03	Windy
May 17	CWOSSA High School/Brantford	1	54.9	49.4		1:59.1	Didn't feel relaxed. 20' between 800 and 400H
May 19	National Camp, Provo, Utah		52.23				Tired from day travel. Took 4 days to recover
May 23	Provo, Utah		52.06 pb		21.78 pm/pb		400H pb by .05 200 pb by .5
May 25/ 26	High School Regionals, Windsor	1	53.1	48.30			
June 1	High School Champ. OFSSA, Etobicoke	1	53.06	48.30			15 strides between hurdles 4 × 400 split 47.2
June 24	London A.C.			48.4	21.7		Felt quick/strong
June 30/ July 1	National Champ. Olympic Trials, Winnipeg	2 3	52.72(h) 51.59(f) pb				Strides 23,14,14 15 to 9 16 & 10. Felt great
July 7	Tillsonburg Invitational	5	51.79				15 strides all the way. Tight hamstring
July 17	Corsaire Invit. Montreal	1				1:49.60 pb	25.5/52.3/1:19./ Tempo all week since hamstring. 3 sec. pb
Aug. 4/5	Ontario OTFA Championships, Kitchener	1	52.32	48.30			Windy. Sick week before
July 22	Nat'l Juniors, Edmonton	2	51.50 pb				14 strides for 3H 15 to 8H 16 in. Messed up H 10
Aug. 20	Miami, Florida, Canada vs USA	3		47.9			4 × 400 split 46.9 windy
Aug. 23	PAN AM Juniors, Nassau, Bahamas	3	52.14				15 strides all the way. Windy, rainy. 1½ hour delay. 2 Americans 1st, 2nd
			12	7	2	3	Total Races
			51.50 (e)	47.9	21.78 (e)	1:49.60 (e)	Best Times (pb's)

162

Table 5-9 Yearly Results Graph

Year 19___   Name_____

Recorded Events <u>Men 400m Hurdles</u>

Higher					
49.60					
49.80					
50.00					
50.20					
50.40					
50.60					
50.80					
51.00					
51.20					
51.40					
51.60					
51.80					
52.00					
52.20					
52.40					
52.60					
52.80					
53.00					
53.20					
53.40					
Lower					

Date, Meet, Places, Comments

The Yearly Plan

Once the data has been gathered and considered, an "Individual Yearly Training Program" or "Chart" must be drawn up. Two sample charts follow. (Tables 5-10 and 5-11). Table 5-10 is a blank chart for an Individual Sport, one of a series designed for the Coaching Association of Canada by Bompa and Denis. The forms are now in wide use by sports governing bodies in Canada. Table 5-11 is a completed chart prepared for Canada's Andrea Page in her quest for a Commonwealth Games medal in 1986. The chart contains: (i) the months and dates of the entire year; (ii) major and minor competitions; (iii) camps, phases of training, number of times per week training; (iv) Pb's at the start of the year; (v) training objectives (goals) and progress.

To compile this chart, the coach starts in Phase V – Specific Competition Phase – and marks in all major and minor competitions. From here, he/she works *backwards* to plan the other phases. All available information about the entire year is included. The length of each phase is set on the needs (strengths and weaknesses) of each individual athlete. Emphasis must be placed on the athlete's objectives for the programme even in the face of distractions which often arise.

The training chart, is a *plan*, rather than a daily record of work done. It is like a blank calendar: it shows the framework of each year and there is space to put dates which are important to each person (Christmas, New Year, parents' anniversary, friends' birthdays). With that framework, the document becomes easy to consult when setting specific objectives (taking holidays, buying gifts, saving money for school). The calendar does not tell a person what to do each day, but it does help to indicate what is appropriate behaviour at any particular time of the year.

Details of each session are designed much closer to the time of training. A week or two in advance is quite sufficient. The athlete's adaptation to previous training must be considered. The coach's ability to monitor, evaluate and react to the athlete's acceptance of training is a far more valuable skill than the mere selection of workouts.

It is a knowledge of the factors which determine the selection of each workout for which the coach must strive. When the components of training (the 5 S's) are correctly combined according to the principles of supercompensation the result is a programme which is naturally periodized for the achievement of specific objectives. From such a programme, the details of each session fall easily into place.

Table 5-12 gives an example of a working document which may be useful for a coach preparing and implementing an Annual Plan for the 100m hurdles. The vertical columns list the components, or aspects of components, which the coach wishes to emphasize, while the horizontal columns indicate the emphasis each component receives during the various phases of the year.

In the sample shown, the author has chosen to remind himself of the basic Power Speed Drills, Speed (including starts), Rhythm (3 and 5 strides) and Strength Endurance.

(While this is an example of the use of the document, it also corresponds exactly with precepts emphasized throughout the book. *Speed* is the number one priority necessary for sprint hurdle success. Next to Speed comes *Hurdle Rhythm*. These are therefore the components set out in the "aide-memoire". Other components (Strength, Tempo, Special Endurance, Flexibility, etc.) are not neglected in day-to-day programming (see Tables 5-14 to 5-20) but it is extremely useful for the coach to be able to remind himself of his priorities at a glance!)

Table 5-10 The Chart of the Yearly Plan (Individual Sport) (Prepared by T. Bompa and R. Denis)

TYPE: COACH: YEAR:

	MONTHS	OCT	NOV	DEC	JAN	FEB	MAR	APR	MAY	JUNE	JUL	AUG	SEPT
DATES	WEEKENDS												
	DOMESTIC												
COMPETITIVE CALENDAR	INTERNATIONAL												
	LOCATION												

	TRAINING PHASE	PHASE I		PHASE II		PHASE III		T	PHASE I			PHASE II		PHASE III	IV	PHASE V	REGENERATION
PERIODIZATION	STRENGTH																
	ENDURANCE																
	SPEED																
	SKILL ACQUISITION																
	PSYCHOLOGICAL																
	MACRO-CYCLES	1	2	3	4	5	6	7	8	9	10	11	12	13	14	
	MICRO-CYCLES	1 2 3 4	5 6 7 8	9 10 11 12	13 14 15 16	17 18 19 20	21 22 23 24	25 26 27 28	29 30 31 32	33 34 35 36	37 38 39 40	41 42 43 44	45 46 47 48	49 50 51 52		

PEAKING INDEX													
TESTING DATES													
MEDICAL CONTROL DATES													
CAMP/SEMI-CAMP													

TRAINING FACTORS	% 100		100%
	1		
	2		
	3		
	4		
	5		
	PEAKING		70%

% 100
90
80
70
60
50
40
30
20
10

VOLUME
INTENSITY ·········
PEAKING

166

Table 5-11 The Chart of the Yearly Plan – Example

Prepared for Andrea Page (Personal Best 57.14 – 400 hurdles) for the 1985-86 year.

■ – major emphasis
▲ – minor emphasis

Table 5-12 A simple Aide-memoire for Periodization (Example 100m Hurdles)

COMPONENT	BASIC DRILLS	SPEED (incl. STARTS)	RHYTHM (3 strides)	RHYTHM (5 strides)	STRENGTH ENDURANCE
NOTES (H = hurdle) PHASE	Power Speed (10 secs/rps) - A,B,C, march, skip, run (with or without H) Mach - leading legs, fast step - trail leg series, dynamic - "Wall attack" with lead leg	Over 1-3 H. (max 5H) Can be with or without H. Can be with harness or accelerator "Speed" - Max 60m	Slightly reduced spacing, low or regular height.	11-11.5 btw. H, low height (76cm). Use sticks, flat H or low H. Use in GDR warm-up (5 strides only)	6-12H regular ht./space lead or trail leg only A's; skips; run "Mixed"; add resistance
PHASE I GENERAL EVENT ADAPTATION	1-5 low H (1.0-3.5m between. Use in w-up for specific needs	Falling starts (20-30m can be submax. for technique. 7.8-8m btw.H	Falling starts (4-6H) 7.2-7.5 btw. H (later 7.5-7.8)	Falling starts (2-4H) 11-11.3 btw. H.	6H (over side of H) Running A's (20-40m) (sandbag optional) (bounding) up to 60m
PHASE II SPECIFIC EVENT ADAPTATION	Reduce frequency	Block starts (3-5H) 80-82 btw.H. (Block or falling starts 21m to first H	Block or falling starts (5-8H) 8.2-8.4 btw.H. (up to 12H possible)	Block or falling starts (4-8H), 11.5 btw. H. (1st H can be at 21m.)	7-12 H Running A's (to 80m)
PHASE III COMPLETE EVENT ADAPTATION	Only if necessary	Block starts (3-5H) 8.3-8.4 btw. H (8.5 if done with opponent)	Racing is Rhythm! Up to 10H, 8.3-8.4 btw. H.	GDR warm-up (5 strides only) Block starts (up to 5H), 11.5-11.8 btw.H	—
PHASE IV BREAK	Use for error correction if necessary	Sprint technique corrections if necess. Keep speed but reduce distance	Use to improve rhythm if necessary.	Block starts (up to 5H) (to correct faults or increase frequency)	6H Running A's (15-20m)
PHASE V SPECIFIC COMPETITION	—	Block starts (2-4H) 8.3-8.4 btw.H. (8.5 if done with opponent)	Racing is Rhythm! Up to 8H, 8.3-8.4 btw. H.	5 strides in warm-up series. Block starts (up to 5H) 11.5-11.8 btw. H.	—
PHASE VI TRANSITION	Skill at leisure	Fun activities and games			↑

As previously mentioned, modern hurdling programmes are generally designed on the basis of a double-periodized year. The basic Matveyev model (Table 5-1) worked backwards from the major competitions at which the intensity of training was high and the volume was low. Volume and intensity were separated throughout entire phases, coming together only as one dropped and the other rose in emphasis.

Whether this in fact was what was happening on the training tracks of the leading hurdlers is open to question, but it did make for a striking, easily explained graph. This had the admirable effect of setting planning for success as a priority in the minds of a generation of coaches world wide.

The experiences of these coaches and their athletes now make it possible to describe a new model. The knowledge of *supercompensation*, especially the role of recovery, and of the *specificity* of the components of training, has led to a periodization model where volume and intensity go much more in parallel. This model, derived from the work of Peter Tschiene, is shown in Table 5-13.

The model is designed for elite athletes and presupposes that the athletes have been in the sport for a number of years. It is dominated by highly specific and intense training. This is made possible by more frequent *recovery* cycles and breaks designed to *prevent* overstress or injury during future loading. There are strong variations in the training (site, mode, etc.) in order to avoid cumulative stress. This in turn allows high loads to be maintained.

The application of this model to 100m hurdle preparation is shown in Table 5-14. Tables 5-15 to 5-21 also use the same principles in providing samples for sprint hurdle and 400m hurdle preparation through the various phases of the year.

Table 5-13 Double Periodization (Based on Tschiene Model)

Month	Oct	Nov	Dec	Jan	Feb	Mar	Apr	May	June	July	Aug	Sept
Period	Preparation Period I				Comp I	Preparation Period II				Competition Period II		
Phase	I		II		III	I		II		III	IV	V	T VI

Volume ▬▬ 100%

Intensity ▪▪▪▪ 80%

Prophylactic Break (Rest) ░░░

170

Table 5-14 Double Periodization Volumes of Work for 100m Hurdles

Month	Oct	Nov	Dec	Jan	Feb	Mar	Apr	May	June	July	Aug	Sept
Period	Preparation Period				Comp	T	Preparation Period			Competition Period		
Phase	I		II		III	T	I	II	III	IV	V	VI
Vol. of Speed			95% + intensity									
Vol. of Tempo (Aerobic)				80% ↓ Intensity								
Vol. of Speed Endurance (rhythm)			95% +									
Vol. of Technique												

171

Table 5-15 Sample Schedule (100/110m Hurdles) – Phase I (General Event Adaptation)

Overview and Objectives

This phase 1 program is designed to: (i) develop and improve total body fitness by improving general aerobic endurance (Tempo), general Strength (circuits), Flexibility; (ii) develop and improve skill (hurdling, sprinting); (iii) identify, evaluate and test individual strengths and weaknesses; (iv) introduce the correct energy systems to maintain submaximal levels of Speed, Speed Endurance (Rhythm); (v) establish alternate warm up procedures; (vi) increase volume of work throughout the phase.

Basic Weekly Structure (microcycle) – (4 week sample)

Week	Day 1				Day 2	Day 3	Day 4		Day 5	Day 6	Day 7
	Harness	Speed	Rhythm	Strength Endurance ("A's")	Tempo (extensive)		Rhythm (5-strides)	Strength Endurance (A's)			
1	2×20m	3×40m	2(4H,5H)	3×50m	20' jog	Sport (Recovery)	4(4H)	2×60m	Recovery	Hills	Rest
2	3×20m	4×40m	3(4H,5H)	4×50m	25' jog		5(4H)	2×70m			
3	4×20m	5×40m	4(4H,5H)	5×50m	30' jog		6(4H)	2×80m			
4	3×20m	4×40m	3(4H,5H)	4×50m (+ circuits)	25' jog (+ wts)		5 (5 stride)	2×70m (+ circuit)			

172

Sample Training Week — (Microcycle) — **Phase I**

Day 1	Day 2	Day 3	Day 4	Day 5	Day 6	Day 7
Warm-up: Part I (skill) Part II (acceleration)	Continuous Warm-up	Warm-Up: Part I	Warm-up: Part I & II	Continuous Warm-Up	Continuous Warm-up or Tempo Warm-up	Rest
Speed + Technique with Harness or Accelerator						
Rhythm with hurdles (sub max)			Rhythm (sub max) (5 stride drills)		Hills (may include skill, speed, speed endurance, tempo, strength endurance)	
Strength Endurance (Circuits, A's)	Tempo (extensive)		Strength Endurance (Circuits, A's or weights)			
Tempo (recovery)	Strength Endurance (weights introduction)	Choice of recovery activity or sport	Tempo (extensive, with recovery)	Recovery activity (modernized ball, pool, dance, sport)	Pool workouts	

173

Table 5-16   Sample Schedule (100/110m Hurdles) – Phase II (Specific Adaptation)

Overview and Objectives

This phase is designed to: (i) enhance event specific training in two ways: a) special intensity, b) race rehearsing; (ii) enhance event specific training to prepare and unite with the competitive phase III; (iii) refine and stabilize technique (event specific skills) and warm-up procedures; (iv) tax and develop the correct energy systems of Speed, Speed Endurance (Rhythm), Tempo by maintaining or increasing volume slightly while increasing intensity; (v) develop Maximum Strength and introducing Special Strength (elastic) more specifically; (vi) educate the correct firing and synchronization of the central nervous system by applying the principles of supercompensation.

Basic Weekly Structure (microcycle) – (4 week sample)

Week	Day 1		Day 2	Day 3	Day 4			Day 5	Day 6		Day 7
	Speed Endurance	Strength Endurance (lead/trail)	Tempo Endurance (extensive)	Recovery	Speed	Speed Endurance	Strength Endurance A's	Tempo Recovery	Speed Endurance	Strength Endurance A's	Rest
1	2(2×8H)	5×8H	15'	Recovery	2(2×2,3H)	3(4H)	4×40m	Warm-up	2(2×100,120)	3×80	Rest
2	2(2×9H)	5×10H	20'	Recovery	2(3×2,3H)	4(6H)	4×40m	Warm-up	2(3×100,120)	4×80	Rest
3	2(2×10H)	5×12H	15'	Recovery	3(2×3H)	5(5H)	4×50m	Warm-up	2(3×80,100)	5×80	Rest
4	2(2×8H)	5×10H	10' (+wts)	Recovery	2(2×3H)	4(6H)	3×50m (+wts)	Warm-up	2(2×80,100)	4×80 (+wts)	Rest
Notes	For recovery refer to Chapter 3				5 Stride 11.0-11.50mH						

174

Sample Training Week — (Microcycle) — **Phase II**

Day 1	Day 2	Day 3	Day 4	Day 5	Day 6	Day 7
Warm-Up Parts I & II	Continuous Warm-Up		Warm-Up Parts I & II		Warm-Up Parts I & II	
Special Strength (20 contacts)			Special Strength			
Technique with Harness or Accelerator	Medicine Ball		Technique with Harness or Accelerator		(Early in phase) Hills (Later in phase) Speed Endurance	
Speed Endurance (Rhythm)			Speed (with hurdles)			
			Speed Endurance (Rhythm)		Speed Endurance (hurdles)	
Strength Endurance (A's, circuit, hurdles)	Tempo (extensive)		Strength Endurance (A's, weights)	Recovery activity		Rest
Tempo (extensive)	Strength (weights)	Continuous recovery activity or sport	Tempo (extensive)	Tempo circuit (sport, medicine ball)	Strength (weights)	

175

Table 5-17 Sample Schedule (100/110m Hurdles) — Phase III (Complete Adaptation – Competition Phase)

Overview and Objectives

This phase is designed to: (i) bring all training components together by increasing intensity and recovery and decreasing volume to bring competitive performance to a peak; (ii) establish the correct number of competitions and correct timing for warm-ups for peaking using supercompensation; (iii) gain self confidence in oneself, race plan and race situations based on successful and stabilized rehearsing (Speed, Speed Endurance (Rhythm)); (iv) maintain levels of Strength Endurance, Strength, Special Strength and Tempo Endurance.

Basic Weekly Structure (microcycle) – (4 week sample)

Week	Day 1				Day 2	Day 3	Day 4	Day 5	Day 6	Day 7
	Speed	Speed Endurance (Rhythm)	Strength (circuit)	Tempo (extensive)	Tempo Endurance (extensive)		Speed			
1	2 × 3,4H	6H, 8H			15'	Rest or Tempo	2 × 2H	Rest	Race	Rest
2	3 × 3,4H	8H, 10H			20'	Rest or Tempo	3 × 2H	Or Warm-Up Parts I & II	Race	Rest
3	3 × 2,3H	6H, 8H			15'	Rest or Tempo	2 × 2H	Race	Rest	
4	2 × 2,3H	8H			10' (+ wts)	Rest or Tempo	2 × 2H	Race	Rest	
Notes	3 stride, 8.4m between Hurdles									

Sample Training Week — (Microcycle) — **Phase III**

Day 1	Day 2	Day 3	Day 4	Day 5	Day 6	Day 7
Warm-Up Parts I, II	Continuous Warm-Up		Warm-Up Parts I, II		Warm-Up Parts I, II	
Harness or Accelerator						
Speed with Hurdles	Medicine Ball circuit		Speed with Hurdles			
Rhythm (short)						
Strength Endurance (upper body circuit)	Tempo (extensive)					
Tempo (extensive)	Weights	Medicine Ball circuit or Tempo on grass	Tempo (extensive)	Rest or Warm-Up Parts I, II	Race or Speed Endurance	Rest

Table 5-18 Sample Schedule (400m Hurdles) — Phase I (General Event Adaptation)

Overview and Objectives

This phase 1 program is designed to: (i) develop and improve general aerobic endurance (Tempo), general Strength Endurance (circuits, A's), Flexibility; (ii) develop and improve sprinting and hurdling skills; (iii) identify, evaluate and test individual strengths and weaknesses; (iv) introduce the correct energy systems to maintain submaximum levels of Speed, Speed Endurance; (v) develop maximum levels of Tempo (extensive and intensive) to prepare for Special Endurance; (vi) establish alternate warm-up procedures; (vii) increase volume of work in a cyclic pattern to ensure basic training principles of periodization allow peaking in later phases.

Basic Weekly Structure (microcycle) – (4 week sample)

Week	Day 1			Day 2		Day 3	Day 4			Day 5	Day 6	Day 7
	Speed Endurance	Tempo Endurance (extensive)	Strength Endurance (A's)	Tempo Endurance (intensive)	Tempo (extensive)	Sport	Speed Endurance	Tempo Endurance (intensive)	Strength Endurance (A's)	Regeneration	Hills	Free
1	2(80,100)	2(3×200)	3×100	10' jog	30' jog	Sport	2(60,70)	1(2,3,4,5)	2(40,50)	Regeneration	Hills	Free
2	3(80,100)	3(3×200)	4×100	15' jog	35' jog	Sport	3(60,70)	1(2,3,4,5,6)	3(40,50)	Regeneration	Hills	Free
3	4(80,100)	4(3×200)	5×100	20' jog	40' jog	Sport	4(60,70)	2(2,3,4,5,6)	3(40,50)	Regeneration	Hills	Free
4	3(80,100)	3(3×300)	4×100 (+circuit)	15' jog	35' jog (+wts)	Sport	3(60,70)	1(2,3,4,5,6)	3(40,50) (+circuit)	Regeneration	Hills	Free

178

Sample Training Week — (Microcycle) — **Phase I**

Day 1	Day 2	Day 3	Day 4	Day 5	Day 6	Day 7
Warm-Up Parts I, II	Warm-Up Part I	Continuous Warm-Up	Warm-Up Parts I & II (skill)	Continuous Warm-Up	Continuous Warm-Up or Tempo	Rest
Speed Endurance (technique)			Speed Endurance (sub max.)			
Tempo (extensive)	Tempo (extensive)		Tempo (intensive)			
Strength Endurance (circuits A's) See Samples	Strength: Introduction to Weights		Strength Endurance (circuits, A's)			
Tempo (with recovery)		Choice of recovery activity or sport	Tempo (extensive – with recovery)	Regeneration Activities	Hills	

179

Table 5-19 Sample Schedule (400m Hurdles) — Phase II (Specific Adaptation)

Overview and Objectives

This phase is designed to: (i) enhance event specific training in two ways: a) special intensity, b) race rehearsing; (ii) enhance event specific training to prepare and unite with the phase III; (iii) refine and stabilize technique (event specific skills) and warm-up procedures; (iv) tax and develop the correct energy systems of Speed, Speed Endurance, Special Endurance 1 and 2 and Tempo by maintaining or increasing volume slightly while increasing intensity; (v) develop Maximum Strength and introducing Special Strength (elastic) more specifically; (vi) educate the correct firing and synchronization of the central nervous system by applying the principles of supercompensation.

Basic Weekly Structure (microcycle) – (4 week sample)

Week	Day 1			Day 2	Day 3	Day 4		Day 5	Day 6		Day 7
	Speed Endurance Warm-ups I, II	Strength Endurance A's	Tempo Endurance (extensive)	Tempo Endurance (extensive)	Free Activity	Special Endurance 1	Strength Endurance	Tempo	Special Endurance 2 Harness	Strength Endurance A's	Rest
1	2(100, 120)	3 × 120	15' jog	(100 + 100 + 100)	Free Activity	3(2 × 200/3H)	3 × 60	Tempo	2(2 × 300/7H)	2 × 40	Rest
2	3(100, 120)	3 × 150	20' jog	100 + 100 +	Free Activity	3(2 × 200/4H)	4 × 60		2(2 × 300/8H)	3 × 40	Rest
3	4(100, 120)	3 × 180	15' jog	200 + 100)	Free Activity	3(2 × 200/5H)	3 × 70		2(2 × 350/9H)	4 × 40	Rest
4	3(100, 120) (harness)	3 × 150 (+ circuit)	20' jog	(100 + 100 + 100) (+ weights)	Free Activity	3(2 × 300/6H) (weights)	4 × 70		2(1 × 400/9H)	3 × 40 (weights)	Rest

180

Sample Training Week — (Microcycle) — **Phase II**

Day 1	Day 2	Day 3	Day 4	Day 5	Day 6	Day 7
Warm-Up Parts I, II			Warm-Up Parts I, II		Warm-Up Parts 1 & 2	
Harness or Accelerator			Special Strength		Harness or Accelerator	
Speed Endurance (with and without hurdles)	Continuous Warm-Up (on grass)		Special Endurance 1 (with and without hurdles)			
Strength Endurance (circuits, A's)	Tempo (extensive)		Strength Endurance	Continuous Warm-Up	Hills (early in phase) or pool work. Special Endurance 2 (later in phase)	
Tempo (extensive, with recovery)	Strength (weights)	Choice of recovery activity or sport	Weights		Strength Endurance (A's, circuits) or weights	Rest
			Tempo (extensive)	Tempo (extensive)		

181

Table 5-20   Sample Schedule (400m Hurdles) – Phase III (Complete Adaptation – Competition Phase)

Overview and Objectives

This phase is designed to: (i) bring all training components together by increasing intensity and recovery and decreasing volume to bring competitive performance to a peak; (ii) establish the correct number of competitions and correct timing for warm-ups for peaking using supercompensation; (iii) gain self confidence in oneself, race plan and race situations based on successful and stabilized rehearsing (Speed, Speed Endurance, Special Endurance, Special Endurance 1 and 2); (iv) maintain levels of Strength Endurance, Strength, Special Strength and Tempo Endurance.

Basic Weekly Structure (microcycle) – (4 week sample)

Week	Day 1			Day 2	Day 3	Day 4			Day 5	Day 6	Day 7
	Speed	Special Endurance 1	Strength Endurance A's	Tempo Endurance (extensive) (grass)	Rest	Speed (technique)	Speed Endurance	Tempo Endurance (extensive) recovery	Rest or Warm Up 1&2	Race or Special Endurance 2	Rest
1	2(3 × 40,50)	2 × 300H	3 × 40	15' jog	Rest	3 × 20	3 × 1,2H	8 × 200	Rest or Warm Up 1&2	Race or Special Endurance 2	Rest
2	2(4 × 40,50)	2 × 300H	4 × 40	20' jog	Rest	3 × 30	2 × 1,2H	8 × 200	Rest or	Race or Special Endurance 2	Rest
3	2(3 × 30,40)	2 × 300H	3 × 40	15' jog	Rest	2 × 30	2 × 2H	8 × 200	Warm Up		Rest
4	2(2 × 30,40)	1 × 300H	2 × 40 (+ Tempo Endurance)	10' jog (weights)	Rest	2 × 20	2 × 2H	8 × 200 (on grass)	1&2		

Sample Training Week — (Microcycle) — **Phase III**

Day 1	Day 2	Day 3	Day 4	Day 5	Day 6	Day 7
Warm-Up Part I	Continuous Warm-Up		Warm-Up Parts 1, 2		Warm-Up Parts I, II	
Accelerator	Medicine Ball		Speed (techniques)			
Speed (accelerations)	Weights		Speed Endurance (with hurdles)			
Special Endurance						
Strength Endurance (A's, circuit-upper body only)			Weights (optional)			
Tempo (extensive)	Tempo (extensive)	Rest or choice of Tempo (on grass)	Tempo (extensive)	Rest or Warm-Up, Parts I, II	Race or Special Endurance 1 or 2	Rest

Table 5-21 Additional Notes for Phase IV, V, VI (all events)

Phase IV (Break)

Overview and Objectives

The program microcycle will follow the same pattern as Phase III. Emphasis will shift to (i) correcting any *minor* race plan errors or technical errors. (MAJOR TECHNICAL CHANGES MUST NOT BE MADE) (ii) a regeneration program to include increased Tempo (on grass, continuous warm-up, pool work) (iii) travel to a major site and settling into a camp situation (changes in climate, diet, time zone, accommodation, sleep patterns).

Phase V (Specific Competition)

Overview and Objectives

The program is identical to Phase III with the following additional considerations: (i) travel to new competitive settings (changes in climate, diet, time zones, accommodation, sleep patterns). (ii) relaxation (increased massage, tempo and psychological preparation designed to create a positive environment).

Phase VI (Regeneration)

Regeneration or rest occurs away from the track, but should take an *active* form (other sports or recreation activities). The phase is used to prepare for the next year using mental and physical activities not related to hurdling.

APPENDIX A

Terminology in Sprint and Hurdle Training by Gerard Mach

"Terms must be strictly defined if training quality and quantity are to be effective"

TERMINOLOGY IN SPRINT AND HURDLE TRAINING

Gerard Mach, Head Coach and High Performance Consultant of the Canadian Track and Field Association, has developed a terminology for the components of sprint and hurdle training which is now standard in Canada and widely recognized elsewhere. Based on sound physiological principles, it enables the coach to focus on and communicate exactly those components of the events which need to be worked on at any point in the training programme.

This unique contribution has been revised and updated to complement this volume and the author and editor express their gratitude for the insight provided. The significant development of Canadian Track and Field in the last dozen years have been a direct result of Gerard's knowledge and leadership

General terms such as speed, maximum speed, speed endurance, tempo endurance, power and strength, are scientifically defined and taught as concepts at high school or university level. Their application and interpretation, however, is often differently used by coaches in their own training terminology and programming.

Coaches use their own explanations which the athlete quickly comes to understand. There is an obvious need for the athlete to know the kind of work which is to be done because of the different results produced by changes in quality and quantity of training.

The matter becomes more complicated and serious misunderstanding can occur when coaches have to communicate with other coaches, athletes or scientists in the course of clinics, training sessions, or through written material. Unless terms are strictly defined, training quality and quantity can be too easy or too intensive, even when done by the same athlete.

This is the problem faced by the author who had to communicate with over 100 athletes and assistant coaches at the national level and later internationally as well. In the mid-fifties he introduced his own terminology system for the sprint and hurdle events based on measurable physical and physiological principles first defined in his Master's thesis. The following discussion identifies components of training which can equally well be applied to event groups other than the sprint and hurdles in which they are widely used at present.

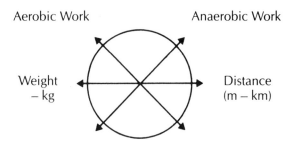

Aerobic Work   Anaerobic Work

Weight – kg   Distance (m – km)

Repetitions – quantity   Time (seconds – hours)

Components

The terminology described identifies twelve *components* of training, each precisely defined. (Coaches familiar with the author's previous work should note an update in the dividing line between Speed and Special Endurance. This update is made necessary by recent research dealt with in the appropriate section.)

1) Speed 1 (Start and Acceleration)	1 – 60m
2) Speed 2 (Maximum Speed Endurance)	60 – 100m
3) Special Endurance 1	100 – 300m
4) Special Endurance 2	300 – 600m
5) Tempo Endurance	up to 600m
6) General Endurance	
7) Strength (Maximum Load)	
8) Power Speed (General)	
9) Power Speed (Mixed)	
10) Strength Endurance (General)	
11) Strength Endurance (Mixed)	
12) Flexibility	

Speed 1 (Start and Acceleration)

This kind of speed work is done over any distance from 1 to 60m reflecting the distance in which most athletes achieve their maximum speed. The 60m distance includes the entire acceleration phase and may or may not include the start. Because speed work from a start position requires more intense and technical work than speed work from a flying start, a distinction is made between speed work with or without starting positions.

The object of each Speed 1 session is to achieve the maximum speed which can be produced that day. Therefore repetitions are limited. Speed 1 work consists of all kinds of accelerations with or without starting positions, both on the track and on downhill slopes. Short accelerations with speed then maintained for the remainder of the 60m may also be included. High knee running is also speed work as long as maximum stride frequency is attained – the "A" exercise for up to 10m at 5 strides per metre is a typical example.

All sessions in the Speed 1 category are anaerobic, with high levels of oxygen debt.

Speed 2 (Maximum Speed Endurance)

Speed 2 deals with distances between 60 and 100m. This is the distance following the acceleration at which maximum speed is attained. The object is to *maintain* the maximum speed and to *slow the rate of deceleration* which then ensues. It was generally thought that even world class athletes could maintain their maximum speed for only about 20m. Controlling the rate of deceleration is therefore important in training. The deceleration rate is less in top athletes than in those at a lower level. Indeed, recent research on Ben Johnson (G. Mach and G. Robertson, May 1986) has shown that he does *not* decelerate in the 100m and it appears that this may also be the case with sprinters like Carl Lewis, Calvin Smith and Chidi Imoh, especially in their best races.

Speed 2 work should be timed and measured. As for Speed 1, repetitions are limited. High knee running at maximum stride frequency may also be included, such as the "A" exercise up to 20m. Hamstring injuries are common at maximum speed so the coach must be very careful to watch for the highest level of running technique and to avoid the runner becoming tense.

It should be noticed that maximum speed endurance can also be developed through other components such as Power Speed, Special Endurance, Strength Endurance and Tempo.

All Speed 2 sessions are anaerobic, with high levels of oxygen debt.

Special Endurance 1

Special Endurance 1 covers distances between 100 and 300m. The distances are run at high speed with minimum deceleration. Performances as high as 14.5 for 150m, 19.7 for 200m and 30.5 for 300m can be achieved.

Any desired distance can be used (120, 130, 140, 150, 200, 220, 250, 300, etc). Special Endurance 1 is an extremely good indicator of the readiness of an athlete to compete at highest level, and in which event.

Only a few repetitions can be made in one training session. Recoveries should last 10 min or more. Although the object is to cover the distance very quickly, coaches should emphasize *control of running* at high speed rather than a fast performance at the expense of control.

Although Special Endurance 1 is an indicator of competitive readiness, it can be introduced throughout the entire annual training program as a form of monitoring. Oxygen debt is very high, as Special Endurance 1 is 90-95% anaerobic and only 5-10% aerobic.

Special Endurance 2

Special Endurance 2 covers distances from 300 to 600m. It is therefore one of the key components for 400m runners and can also be useful in identifying 800m potential. Former world record holders in the 800m such as Fiasconaro, Juantorena and Zlateva have emphasized Special Endurance 2, while competing at 400m and training mainly in the 400 – 200m program. On the other hand, Irena Szewinska did not include Special Endurance

2 in her program because it was felt that she could still improve her 100m. (For this reason, Special Endurance 1, Tempo work up to 300m, and Strength Endurance replaced Special Endurance 2 in her program.) Coaches must appreciate that an emphasis on Special Endurance 2 work will have some negative effect on results in shorter distances and should use other components if this problem is to be avoided.

One or two repetitions with a recovery of 10 min or more is sufficient for a Special Endurance 2 session. (As an example, Juantorena did 2x600m in 1:15 with a 10 min recovery five days before the 1976 Olympics. Zlateva did similar workouts in 1972.)

Special Endurance 2 can be introduced throughout the annual training program either as training or as a test in the form of a "time trial". It is most useful in monitoring the results of other components such as Tempo and in indicating any necessary changes in intensity or quantity.

Hurdlers should do Special Endurance 2 work, with hurdles up to 400m and without hurdles up to 600m.

Oxygen debt is very high as Special Endurance 2 is 80-85% anaerobic and 15-20% aerobic.

Tempo Endurance

Tempo Endurance covers any distance up to 600m. It can be done in many different ways, with varying distances, intensities, recoveries and on different surfaces.

The underlying principle of Tempo Endurance does not change, however. The emphasis is on the *quantity* of running. It is certainly possible for the work to be done at a range of speed which may become quite fast as the Tempo Endurance prepares for the transition into Special Endurance work. Distance and quantity are adjusted for the athlete, the event and the training period. In the sprint and hurdle events, the distances used are the same as in Speed and Special Endurance 1 and 2 components.

Distances and number of repetitions have to be carefully planned by the coach. The variables are the distance, the number of repetitions, the speed and the recovery. When Tempo work is timed, it should be monitored by the coach.

There are a number of methods of structuring Tempo Endurance.

Untimed

1. Untimed repetitions
    100 + 100 + 150 + 150 + 100
    or 150 + 150 + 200 + 200 + 150
    or 150 + 150 + 300 + 300 + 150
    or 150 + 300 + 600 + 300 + 150
    or 150 + 300 + 600 + 600 + 600 + 300 + 150

+ indicates a 100m jog at the athlete's own pace. As can be seen, repetitions can be varied to suit any needs. Arrangements such as pyramids (200-300-500-300-200) are as acceptable as repetitions of the same distance.

2. "Intervals"

The author has used the term in this context to describe distances *broken down into smaller sections* with a very brief recovery consisting simply of slowing down and turning around. This is often easier psychologically on athletes who may have difficulty handling such workouts as 5 x 600. Using the interval method, this would be broken down by the coach into five sets of 6 x 100 for a similar, but more efficient training effect. Other examples are 10 (4 x 50), 6(3X100).

Timed

Repetitions of a planned distance (e.g. 6 x 300m in 36 seconds with a 5 minute recovery)

Timed Tempo Endurance can also be used to make the transition to Special Endurance. For example, an athlete could progress from 8 to 6 to 4 to 3 x 300 over four workouts. The increase in speed for the fixed quantity of running indicates the athlete's readiness for Special Endurance. The optimal point in Tempo work has been reached when the athlete can do the running within about 15% of the Special Endurance time.

Tempo Endurance is a component designed to improve Special Endurance. It does not directly and automatically prepare an athlete for competition. An athlete who can run 6 x 300m in 35 seconds may not yet be ready to race the 300m distance in 33.0. The specific preparation work necessary is done with Special Endurance 1.

Tempo work in Phase I of the preparation program will be performed close to aerobic levels. The intensity will gradually increase to almost total anaerobic work.

This progression of Tempo from aerobic to anaerobic should be evident to coaches because all sprint events are fundamentally high in oxygen debt. An athlete can therefore prepare at his/her highest level only following anaerobic preparation. Controlled Special Endurance in the form of time trials can help avoid training mistakes and disappointments (when an athlete for example has relied too heavily on aerobic preparation).

General Endurance

General Endurance or aerobic work has a limited effect on sprint results (in contrast to its effect on distance results). This means that a limited percentage of the training percentage will be spent on the development of General Endurance. The shorter the distance run in competition, the less effect of General Endurance training on the results.

Normally, sprinters will have a sufficient amount of General Endurance in the warm-up, in easy Tempo and the type of active rest provided by jogging during recoveries. 200 and 400m runners need some General Endurance in their programs, but it is not a major component in any training phase.

Through development of a higher maximum oxygen uptake, General Endurance leads to quicker recovery after intensive training. It also allows the athlete to increase his or her work load. Nevertheless, General Endurance should not be overestimated in the sprints. General Endurance work is wholly aerobic.

Strength

Muscle strength is required by sprinters, particularly 100m runners during the start and the acceleration. Strength training with heavy loads improves the capacity of the muscles to perform heavy work, but it does not automatically improve their muscle speed. Not all throwers, usually very strong, are fast. Not even all strong sprinters are very fast. Moreover, even some world class sprinters are not tremendously fast from the starting blocks and probably never could be (Irena Szewinska, Alberto Juantorena, Steve Williams, Don Quarrie, and Tommy Smith are examples).

Speed is a neuro-muscular action, and therefore fast reaction, technique and coordination are required. Some athletes such as Borsov and Larry James (silver medal, 1968 Olympic 400m, 43.9 sec) needed no heavy weight training in their programs. Borsov limited his strength work to testing situations.

The type of athlete who reacts well to strength training is the one who is already powerfully built and has decided to compete in the 60 and 100m events. For example, getting from a quarter squat to full extension with maximum load on a squat rack requires an action which is similar to a sprinter leaving the blocks. One hundred percent concentration is required and the maximum number of muscle fibres must be recruited without tension to accelerate the weight from rest as quickly as possible.

The personal coach has the responsibility to design a long-term and short-term strength program taking the requirements of the particular athlete and desired event into consideration.

The Strength component includes all heavy weight work comprising weight from 50% body weight to maximum. There should be no more than five repetitions of any exercise. All kinds of weight lifting can be done, including the use of the special heavy load or resistance machines now available.

All Strength work with heavy loads is performed anaerobically.

Power Speed (with weights or resistance machines)

For exercises to be defined as Power Speed, load and repetitions have to be limited. Repetitions are limited to 10, the time to 10 seconds, and the load is limited to 50% of body weight. Load, however, is adjusted to the requirements of a particular athlete to allow the exercise to be executed with acceptable speed and rhythm. There would, however, be a difference in training load between heavier athletes like Bob Hayes, Allan Wells, Haseley Crawford, Alberto Juantorena, Renate Stecher, Angella Issajenko and Ben Johnson, and lighter ones such as Don Quarrie, Steve Williams, Tommy Smith, Angela Bailey, Marita Payne, Irena Szewinska, etc.

Provided the restrictions on load and duration are observed, all weightlifting work, including that done with load or resistance machines, can be included in the Power Speed component. Power Speed with weights is a preparation component which does not have an automatic effect on results.

Because time and repetitions are limited, Power Speed with weights is done anaerobically.

Power Speed (Mixed)

Power Speed (mixed) is the name given to exercises performed under the same conditions as the section above, but without weights or machines. It can be done with loads such as sandbags or weight jackets from 8 to 12 kg, or medicine balls from 3 to 5 kg. It can be done also with resistance provided by hills, water, sand, snow, treadmills, etc.

It will be recalled that the distance over which the exercise is done does not exceed 20m. Repetitions do not exceed ten, and each repetition does not take more than 10 sec.

Power Speed (mixed) has been identified as extremely related to an effective sprinting action in technique and in physiological intensity. Exercises should be done with ideal technique to achieve maximum effectiveness.

The most effective exercises for Power Speed (mixed) are those which include all or most of the elements of sprinting. These are:

• high knee marching – A, B exercises
• high knee skipping – A, B exercises
• high knee running – A, B exercises
• bounding
• (for hurdles) the C exercises at a march, skip or run.

Power Speed (mixed) work can be included in all stages of a sprint and hurdle program. Because of the speed with which the exercises are done and the limited time, repetition and distance, Power Speed (mixed) exercises are anaerobic in nature.

Strength Endurance (with weights or resistance machines)

Strength Endurance and Power Speed use the same exercises. The critical difference lies in the load, the duration and the quantity. The load on Strength Endurance exercises is limited to a maximum of 50% body weight and there is no limit to time or quantity except that which is necessary for each athlete to maintain correct execution.

The value of Strength Endurance exercises lies in the fact that sprint and hurdle events are not made up of one explosive action like jumps or throws. Rather they are repetitions of intense cycles of action.

Strength Endurance with weights is a preparation for more specific components. An improvement in Strength Endurance weight work does not automatically bring with it an improvement in race results or even in Strength Endurance (mixed). Coaches should therefore use it as general preparation for other components. At the beginning of a program a goal should be established, a desirable quantity with correct execution. Coordination is lost if correct execution is not maintained.

Strength Endurance (mixed)

Following the general guidelines for Strength Endurance noted above, the same exercises are used in Strength Endurance (mixed) as in Power Speed (mixed). If loads are used, they can be the same (below 50% body weight, as long as correct execution can be maintained). The major difference is the distance and time over which the exercises are performed. The distance is always more than 20m and the time taken is more than 10 seconds.

400m runners can expect to aim for 200m Strength Endurance, taking perhaps 6 to 7 minutes at 5 strides per metre. 200m runners should aim for 120m (approx 4 min) while 100m runners should aim for 80m (approx 2½ min).

Repetitions will depend on the athlete, the training program and the exercise used. Repetitions can vary as in a "pyramid" (40-80-120-200-120-80-40). Athletes work to the point of exhaustion in both quantity and intensity.

Nevertheless, it is important to point out that the achievement of the prescribed distance is not the major emphasis. Strength Endurance (mixed) exercises should always be observed and *stopped* when the athlete cannot maintain the correct technique. Fatigue will cause the same problems as in 200m and 400m races: low knee lift, backward lean, lowered centre of gravity and loss of ability to run tall (as the supporting leg fails to straighten), loss of rhythm or speed and a general feeling of inability to reach the finish line!

The object of the exercise is to maintain the desirable aspects of technique over distances and times greater than those required in the race.

Done correctly it is the toughest physical work a sprinter or hurdler has in the training program and also gives an excellent psychological preparation for the physical stresses of competition. For all these reasons, it is being used more and more by middle and long distance runners as well.

In principle it is an anaerobic activity, but because of the duration there is considerable aerobic fuelling.

Flexibility

Flexibility is a component which facilitates and improves complex movements and skills. The skill work of not just sprinters, but all track and field athletes is enhanced. Hurdlers, expecially in the 110m hurdle event, must definitely include stretching and flexibility in their programs.

Flexibility is best developed at the earliest possible age before the cross section of the muscle gets too large and the resulting strength inhibits the stretching potential. In gymnastics and figure skating where flexibility is most important for the necessary skills, competitors begin flexibility work as early as three years old. Flexibility at 8 to 12 years old will definitely benefit those who will later turn to hurdles. More can be achieved in a few months at a young age than in years with older athletes. In some cases no improvement can be gained at this stage.

It is because of the early development of flexibility that no top class 400m hurdler has come to excel in the 110m hurdles whereas sprint hurdlers (like Hemery or Akii-bua) have developed into Olympic winners and world record holders in the longer race.

A lot of flexibility is included in the Power Speed and Strength Endurance (mixed) components. If required, however, this can be supplemented by an emphasis on flexibility in the warm up. The duration may be of any length and depending on the execution, it can be aerobic or anaerobic.

Conclusion

The terminology described above allows for a great variety of workouts to be designed in each component. The components are separated by specific use of established measurement units of time, distance, duration and load, as well as of established physiological terms such as aerobic and anaerobic.

The description does not describe all existing methods nor those which will be developed in the future. Nevertheless, each existing method (and future ones) can still be classified according to the components described. The terminology has already been used in the sprint and hurdle programs of many countries. It was first introduced in Canada in January 1973, interpreted into English by Ken Porter and Roger Burrows (then of the Alberta Track and Field Association) on the occasion of Gerard Mach's inaugural Canadian presentation. More and more of the terms are being used in other event groups.

Knowledge of the terminology makes it possible to communicate coaching material and training sessions much more effectively both in written and verbal form between coaches and from coach to athlete. It is still up to the coach to decide which components will be used, when and how, taking into account the varied needs of the athlete in the context of an entire training program.

APPENDIX B

Around the World of Hurdling: selected readings

"Without the heart, there would be no desire to get there; without the brain, there would be no knowing how to get there."

The medalists from the 1986 Commonwealth Games in Edinburgh

(l-r)				
	Colin Jackson	(WALES)	13.42	2nd
	Mark McKoy	(CANADA)	13.31	1st
	Dan Wright	(AUSTRALIA)	13.64	3rd

SELECTED READINGS FROM AROUND THE WORLD OF HURDLING

The readings which follow are reprinted or excerpted from previous publications which give a unique perspective on hurdling, hurdle coaching and hurdlers.

The Women's 100m Hurdles	Tadeusz Szczepanski (Trans. Gerard Mach)
Calvesi	Brent McFarlane
And my dream came true...	Tatiana Anisimova (Trans. Alan Adamson) (Trans. Alan Adamson)
400 Hurdles: a Collection of Scientific Investigation	
Level of Aspiration of Superior Athletes	Brent McFarlane
The Autogenic Way	Brent McFarlane

THE WOMEN'S 100M HURDLES

By Tadeusz Szczepanski, Polish National 100m Hurdles Coach. Translated by Gerard Mach, National Program Director – CTFA. Edited by Brent McFarlane and Roger Burrows. *This is an address given to the 1981 European Coaches Conference in Venice.*

This event is an evolution of sprinting. A female hurdler should be a *"special"* type sprinter having relatively the same talent components:

1. psycho-physical factors
2. motor-movement (elastic strength/power)
3. exercises – efficient nerve-system manifested by a higher degree of flexibility and coordination

The 100m hurdle event in regards to the physical (speed of movement) and physiological aspects (ie. phospho-glycolitic requirements) is considered a sprint event.

The running technique of the hurdle event evolved from the sprint event and two factors characterize the modification of basic sprinting:

1. Speed between the hurdles
2. Speed across the hurdles

As the running part between the hurdles is in a straight line and is derived from the 100m sprint the inner structure of the movement is similar. However, the hurdle stride *appears* to look different than the normal running stride.

The difference is based on the complicated asymmetrical movement of the rear leg and leading leg.

The rear leg moves forward in a compound movement at many different levels in comparison to the normal running stride which is directed only in the horizontal plane.

In order to move the leg over the hurdle without any collision in the most economical and fastest way, the thigh should be taken sideways to an extent determined by the height of the hurdle while retaining the other elements of the movement of sprinting technique.

In other words, it is a sprint stride but executed at compound levels.

The situation is similar with the lead leg, which is more closely related to the sprint stride than the rear leg. The lead leg moves only in the horizontal plane. The difference is in the higher knee lift of the lead leg and the leg extension during the hurdle clearance.

The above mentioned elements describe the hurdle technique in a general model with some individual differences depending on the individual.

One should avoid copying any fixed method in order to use the optimal potential of the athlete.

* * * * * * * *

For better understanding the essence of the 100m hurdle training and the exact method which has been used by the Polish athletes I would like to explain to you what kind of coaching problems I have met and how I resolved them after I became the National Hurdle Coach. The most visible and simple way in which one could achieve some information and make first analysis was to compare the parameters of the old 80m hurdle event and the current 100m hurdle event.

Firstly a very difficult problem for athletes and coaches was the distance between the hurdles, 8.5m. In order to run between the hurdles in a relaxed 3 stride rhythm and with maximal stride frequency, the athlete should have excellent *strength* and *jumping preparation*.

The strength training, a fundamental component in the development of speed and technique, was the first element to emphasize. This is perhaps why experienced hurdlers and multiple event athletes adapted very fast to the new distance.

It seemed to me that the new hurdle height might make it more difficult so that changes in the hurdle technique had to be made. The first season proved changes were not necessary. It was interesting that athletes with better strength preparation could run the hurdles in the same way as before.

It has been *confirmed* that two elements decide the results of modern 100m hurdle training:

1. Special Strength – jumping
2. Speed – rhythm

By emphasizing the direction of these components the training method of Polish hurdlers has been shown. (ie. Rabstyn, Larger, Perka).

In order to convince you I would like to provide you with materials in a simple way in the form of separate studies of motor-components: strength, speed, endurance and technique.

Strength

Strength is a motor-component which in the sprint and hurdle events should be in first place in the overall training process.

The above mentioned statement is correct because:

1. Women generally are approx. 40% weaker than men which determines the type of work which should be done in the preparation period.
2. Strength is the base to build other motor-components (technique, etc.).

In order to work out a strength training program for a female athlete the following items should be taken into consideration:

1. The level of general strength at the beginning.
2. The morphological (anatomical) type of athlete. Body structure problems especially vertebrae in the hip area often cause problems for women.
3. Imbalances in strength of given muscle groups.
4. Individual reactions of the body to strength training such as muscular apathy and neuro-muscular coordination disorders.

Taking into consideration the above mentioned components one can answer the following questions:

1. What kind of strength should be used?
2. How frequent should training sessions be?

Only then can you apply the optimal training method and correct training principles. The basic training elements for hurdlers and sprinters to develop their potential are not different.

One topic is the need for general and dynamic strength training. Strengthening the hip, for example, has an effect in improving the hurdle technique. (The flexors and extensors of the hip joints as well as the group of thigh abductors and adductors.)

The next problem is the work to develop the jump component, which I consider to be a derivative of dynamic strength.

My feeling is that dynamic strength is the No. 1 training component for female hurdlers which I have stressed in my training program. As I mentioned in the introduction the jump component makes it possible to overcome the 8.5m between the hurdles with maximum frequency of stride.

Achieving maximum speed in the hurdle race is possible through maximum stride frequency and maintaining an unchanged length of the strides.

In addition the hurdle stride will be done at full speed without disturbance in the running structure. This requires the necessary power provided by the jump component.

The Method of Strength Training
1. General strength training (max.)
2. Dynamic strength training (special)
3. Jump component training (jump exercises)

In a female training program, *general strength* development has many controversial views (at least in the physiological aspect). Special danger can occur in exercises with weights on the shoulders. It deepens the inborn lordosis and causes pain because of pressure on the nerve-system in the spine (sacro-ilizo joint). This fact is very important in hurdle training in which the specific hip movement of driving the hurdle stride puts more load on that part of the vertebrae.

Table 1 Maximum General Strength

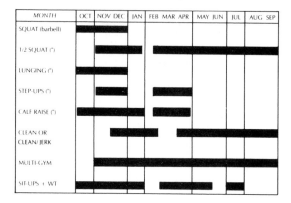

The above mentioned exercises because of their high level stimulus on the whole movement system (bone-joint-muscle system) should be applied 1-2 times a week with a larger number of repetitions or 3-4 times a week with less repetitions. My opinion is that this training is indispensable, since it fires the most of the motor units as well as improves maximum strength.

It seems to me that more frequently one should use training modalities with maximum weights but in isolated positions as with the multiple-gym etc.

Table 2 Dynamic Special Strength

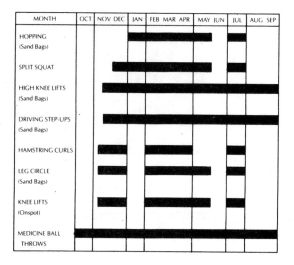

Dynamic Strength (Power) (Special Strength)

This kind of strength is strictly related to the hurdle event. The load (small or medium) should be determined by the ability to *execute the movement at high speed*. It is important that the training in their internal or external structure have several elements of the event-specific movement.

Within each microcycle this kind of strength might be introduced in isolation or as an element of compound training linked together with other components such as speed or hurdle technique.

Jump Training Component

The meaning and importance of this component has been described in my introduction. I present the following materials which develop the jump component in the yearly training program.

Table 3 Jumping Dynamic Power

MONTH	OCT	NOV DEC	JAN	FEB MAR APR	MAY JUN	JUL	AUG SEP
BOUNDING		■	■	■	■	■	■
HOPPING		■	■	■	■	■	■
DOUBLE LEG BOUNCE (over hurdles)	■	■	■	■	■	■	■
SKIP (Locked knee)	■	■		■	■		
DOUBLE LEG BOUNCE (no hurdles)	■	■	■	■	■	■	■

A very effective exercise is bounding on one leg, both left and right, but it should not be the only one. As always in the training program, the best effect will be achieved in a compound program using a variety of exercises.

Speed – Hurdle Rhythm

The next motor component which is important in the sprint events as well as in the hurdles is to improve maximum (absolute) speed.

The speed of a single movement depends on the reaction of the nervous system. This is an inborn factor and can only in a small degree be improved through training.

What can be achieved in speed training is to improve the running technique and the nerve-muscle coordination based on previous preparation of specific dynamic strength and the jump component.

In the sprint and hurdle events, the method to improve maximum speed in principle is similar.

There is, however, a difference in the objective of the speed work. In sprints, the speed work is the final aim, whereas in hurdles, speed work is a stage, a necessary condition. Speed in hurdles requires further work in order to develop into the speed which can be used in running form between the hurdles. The difference is very important and if not understood will lead to serious errors by coaches in developing this hurdle component.

In sprints the relation of the recovery phase and the supporting phase is about 40% greater than to the similar phases of the strides between hurdles.

This fact has its fundamental importance in the hurdle training. If the maximum speed has not been adapted to the hurdle event, then simply, it will never be used 100%.

The first training phase is to improve the running technique through power speed exercises and accelerations. The second training phase is tempo work with changing speed of sub-maximum (97-98%) speed work from 30-50m. Do some individual starts from the starting blocks.

For hurdlers the first training phase can be connected with rhythm work over sticks or cross bars, in order to adapt maximum speed to the hurdles over the same distances as in sprinting (30-50m). In the final training phase (competition) one can introduce a stimulus to achieve over max. speed: run downhill, with wind or specially organized drills.

Endurance

As in the speed component, there are different aims for sprinters and hurdlers when it comes to endurance training.

For sprint events the final aim is to achieve special endurance (speed endurance) but for the hurdle events it is only an important preparation phase. Hurdle endurance (rhythm) is the final aim for the sprint hurdles.

Training phases for sprinters and hurdlers as well as training variables are the same.

The first training phase is the development of general endurance. The second training phase is the development of tempo endurance. The third training phase is the development of speed endurance (special endurance). The rhythm endurance program begins in the second training phase and reaches its height during the pre-competition and competition period.

Hurdle Technique

Now, I am coming to the final but most important component: hurdle technique.

The hurdle race technique should be divided in two elements:

1. The hurdle stride (clearance)
2. Running technique between the hurdles (rhythm)

Regarding the first point, I explained already at the beginning in detail.

In training sessions with my athletes separate exercises of the leading leg or trail leg as well as both legs are used.

The first kind of exercises are hurdle exercises running on the outside of the hurdles with the leading leg or trail leg over the hurdles in one stride rhythm over 6-10 hurdles.

The second kind of exercises are complex exercises such as:

1. Running over the middle of the hurdle in one stride rhythm (the number of hurdles as mentioned above)
2. Marching over the hurdles alternately left-right, 6-10 hurdles(A's, B's)
3. Skipping over the middle of the hurdle in one, two or three strides over 6-10 hurdles (A's, B's)

Now, I would like to describe more regarding the training of rhythm work. This component is the *most important* one in the hurdle training since it comprises the complex subject of running and hurdling.

The training program seeks to improve in two directions:

1. Rhythm – speed
2. Rhythm – endurance

Most important and most difficult to achieve is rhythm endurance (which for hurdle events is special endurance, and for the sprint events speed endurance). The most important period to develop this component is the pre-competition and competition period since the intensity will be the highest.

In the preparation period some medium intensity runs can be used to develop hurdle rhythm eg. little technique, characterized in slower motion, easy hurdle specifications (low hurdle, shorter distances between).

For a good hurdle training method the following elements should be considered:

Modifications to :
1. Hurdle specifications (height of the hurdle and distance between the hurdles)
2. Speed
3. Kind of rhythm (number of strides between the hurdles)
4. Distance and number of hurdles

Table 4 Summary

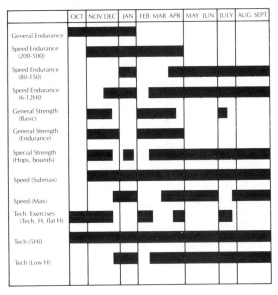

The knowledge to deal with the above mentioned elements will have a decisive role in the effectiveness of the rhythm training. Although there are some principles in which the order should be during the training process, nevertheless, no uniform scheme should be fixed. The effectiveness is related to the progress of the athletes, but one should not omit the next training phase.

For example, without mastering the rhythm over the low hurdles and shorter distances between the hurdles one should not begin further training on more difficult specifications (hurdle height, distance between the hurdles) since the preparation period would be longer and less effective.

In conclusion I would like to express my disappointment that this beautiful female event has been developed properly only in four European countries: Poland, GDR, USSR and W. Germany.

If through my expressed experiences I have brought you a little closer to the 100m hurdle event, it gives me great satisfaction to take part in this way in the development of the event in other countries in Europe.

CALVESI

Italian Alessandro Calvesi was a coaching legend who was in a large part responsible for Guy Drut's 1976 gold medal in the hurdles. See Bibliography Item 72. This is a condensed version of the original article.

"If I have a good piano player and I want to make him great, I must add something. He is not an artist yet, not until everything becomes automatic. Each year, Guy Drut did not start over. He continued his preparation, correcting and building from the weaknesses of the previous year. It took 8 to 10 years to win the Olympic gold medal in Montreal in the 110 metre hurdles." Alessandro Calvesi, August, 1980.

For three days I had asked questions, made notes, listened and admired at what was happening. I had become a student of a man who in the 1960's and 70's had become a legend in hurdle coaching. He had become my friend and teacher. He gave me a unique insight into the hurdle events that showed me why coaches from across Europe still come to him. He was a man of class and a solid personality. His indepth knowledge of hurdling rang out every time he spoke or demonstrated different versions of hurdling drills. Considering he is almost 70 and speaks very little English this experience is one that must be shared with others.

Who is Alessandro Calvesi? The name means very little to the Canadian Track and Field world. We know very little about the European hurdling scene. Gerard Mach, the National Program Director (CTFA) has given us a unique insight into what is involved in sprint-hurdle preparation. We are indeed fortunate to have him in Canada. Calvesi belonged to simpler era of sport, one he calls "natural and not synthetic." He is quick to point out that decathlete Jim Thorpe had his Olympic gold medal taken away from him for being a professional but today athletes are receiving thousands of dollars to compete in international competitions. He is a coach, who had not one, but three hurdlers in the 1964 Tokyo Olympic 110 metre hurdle final and two in the 400 metre hurdle final – a feat never duplicated. His athletes set World, Olympic and European records. Have you ever heard of Filliput, Morale or Otto? He was the man behind Guy Drut (France), the 1976 110 metre Olympic hurdle champion. Now retired, he had been a director and professor at the Institute of physical education in Milan as well as a chief hurdle coach for Italy for over 20 years. He now lives in Brescia with his wife and "translator", Gabré, a two time Olympian herself.

The extent and use of drugs (steroids) for athletics brings a strong response from Calvesi: "If you give steak to one athlete and not another, it is not fair ... but the world goes on. One must set rules even if you don't like them. You must make up your own mind on the limits of doping. New rules are needed."

The boycott of the 1980 Moscow Olympics left many unanswered questions about "who is the number one track and field power in the world?" Many will say the United States while others look to the USSR or GDR. Calvesi makes a number of good points. "Until 1976 the United States had a monopoly on the men's sprint hurdle event. Guy Drut broke the monopoly. If the United States continues to use only the naturally talented athlete and does not train properly, they will lose. The USSR and GDR are good. A natural athlete with good (chemical) assistance and a proper training program will take over. It has been coming for some time. Time will tell the tale." The dominance of the women's 100 metre hurdles by the USSR, GDR and Poland speaks for itself.

What about the Olympic movement and professionalism? Calvesi feels that, "in four to eight years the Olympics should be open to all. Today for an athlete to reach the top he/she must train five to six hours a day and not work. They have to live and be paid for this in some manner. Day by day, athletes become more professional. To make an Olympic final an athlete must train twice a day. Women are training like men. To run 30 km a day takes time. Any woman who trains 5 to 6 hours a day and has ability can't help but be good."

New synthetic tracks through the world have brought about improvements in running surfaces, change in shoe styles, improved performances and the greater chance of injury. Improved surfaces brought about changes in thought about preparation for the hurdle events. "Many of the world's top athletes still train on natural surfaces.

Fewer injuries occur on grass and cinders. Valeri Borsov (USSR) trained on grass and did only maximum intensity work on the synthetic track. Marita Koch (GDR) trains primarily on a cinder track since it feels good for her legs and ankles." It is interesting to note that many tracks in the USSR have a lane of saw dust around them for warming up and to do special jumping and running exercises. Why? You must have strong feet and ankles. Calvesi also stressed this same point when discussing the trail leg for the hurdle take-off and lead leg upon landing.

"Autogenic training" or the use of relaxation through simple methods of hypnosis is a science in many countries. It was reported that the entire GDR track and field team could be seen in Moscow doing a session of autogenic training in an open park near the village. "This type of preparation brings together everything towards that ultimate goal – the Olympic gold medal. You must know where you are at every moment." Calvesi goes on to use a simple analogy related to hurdling.

"The top athletes in the world have a sense of rhythm, in the musical sense. The good ones can't run without this hurdle music. How many times have you heard how easy it was to set a world record? How many athletes remember the events that took place in the race? Ask Moses, Nehemiah, Drut, Komisova or Schaller to remember details." Autogenic training or being simply psyched up! Is there a difference? Many roads lead to Rome. Some countries are leaving nothing to chance and putting to good use, this controlling of the mind.

Many coaches and athletes in Canada in the sprint-hurdle events have become obsessed with the Mach A, B and C warm up drills. Since the warm up is such an intricate part to an entire workout, I asked Calvesi two key questions: What would he suggest for a warm up for the hurdle events? In watching athletes from the GDR, they took an hour and a half to warm up. That involved 45 minutes of jogging and stretching, 20 minutes of flat out sprinting up to 100 metres, very little hurdling, 20 minutes of sitting quietly and then a 400m hurdle race. Why so long and very little 400m hurdle race rehearsing?

"To answer your question, think of the Olympic games or any other international competition. Athletes do their warm up and then are called to report in 20 to 25 minutes before their race. They then are told to sit in a confined area until race time and then receive only 5 minutes on the track to do final preparation for the race. The athletes from the GDR rehearse this constantly. The specifics of the warm up involves easy jogging and loosening up, followed by dynamic (movement) flexibility and running over the sides and middle of hurdles. Twenty-five minutes before the competition we usually do 1 x 1 hurdle and 1 x 4 to 5 hurdles. Never work too hard in the warm up and never be tired. Keep warm and fresh in the final moments before competition. Also remember, the warm up follows as you train. If you train for 3 to 4 hours a day, what is an hour to an hour and a half warm up?"

While sitting in the plane returning to Canada, I thought of Calvesi. His name made me think of a 16th Century Italian artist. I remembered the final hours with Gabré and him in a small Brescia cafe trying to get answers for too many questions. He had said, "you must come back. The time has been too short." How true. He answered all my questions honestly. He took me to meet his family, friends and showed me his land. He treated me to hospitality I never expected. I began to ask myself the question "Why"? Two thoughts came to mind. Firstly, I was a coach! When I had arrived in Italy, I simply phoned him and asked if we might meet and talk. That's all. The fact that I was a coach interested in learning was enough to open the door to this man. Not the case in Canada. I received the same treatment in Finland, West Germany and Scotland. Coaches are special! Secondly, Calvesi was an artist. A real life 20th Century artist.

Postscript

Dear Editor,

In your last issue of 'Ontario Athletics' I wrote the article 'Calvesi' to try to explain the feelings I had after meeting a great man. These feelings were almost impossible to describe, but they were the combination of friendship, honesty and written from the heart. Calvesi died November 28, 1980. I was indeed fortunate to meet this unique, individual and his death is a personal loss to me. The article serves an untimely tribute to a friend.

Brent McFarlane, Kitchener

"AND MY DREAM CAME TRUE"

The ups and downs of a 21 year athletic career!

by Tatiana Anisimova (USSR)
Translated from Legaya Athletika by Alan Adamson,
edited by Brent McFarlane. See Bibliography Item
86.

*The following article will touch all those who have tried
their hardest to reach a goal and fallen short. That which
separates success and failure is a fine line. The mark of a
champion is one who has the ability to come back ... and
come back ... Such is the story of Tatiana Anisimova.*

Much water has flowed under the bridge since my first
involvement in sports. In the past two years I have had
two anniversaries: 1980 marked the 20th year since my
first workout and 1981, 10 years since I joined the USSR
national team. It is with joy and sadness that I look back
over those years. It is still hard to think about that first
anniversary in 1980 when I left the Olympic Village in
tears after my failure. The second one is coloured with
the joy of my World Cup victory in Rome. Now my 22nd
sporting season is beginning and I am closer to the time
of retirement. It is time to sum up what I've done in sports.

For each athlete there are two "scales" of evaluation.
One involves the results, titles, victories and laurels.
These are objective indices. The other is a subjective analysis of one's own actions. Can we find some type of objective criteria here? To me the answer is yes! Ask yourself
the following. Did the dreams you had at the start of your
sporting life come true? If they haven't all come true, did
you do everything possible to bring them about? If you
can answer positively, you have no reason to reproach
yourself, for your sporting activity was not in vain.

I was born in October, 1949 in Grozn. When I was 11,
I began to take an interest in sports. My physical education teacher brought me into track and field and taught
me to love running. He had no intentions of making me
into a high level athlete, but simply to help me become
healthy, strong and agile, so I would stay in sports for a
long time. He strongly felt that we should learn to set our-
selves goals and struggle to achieve them. I recall him

asking me, "What are your dreams?" I wrote, "I dream of competing at the Olympic Games". Why I wrote that I cannot even say today. In any case, no one noticed any special talent in me and I never had very good results. For six years I trained as a pentathlete and of all the events, I most disliked hurdling because women ran 80m hurdles and I was always too cramped between them. I liked sprinting and long jumping and it was in jumping that I got my first success, becoming a candidate for a Master of Sport in 1968. In recalling those adolescent days, I must say words of thanks to my first coach, Alexei Nikolaevich for getting me firmly placed on the sporting path.

Editor's note: In the Soviet Union there is a sports-ranking system designed to help coaches to spot promising athletes with specific targets in mind. A whole complex of qualifying standards, rankings and titles exists for most recognized sports. The Master of Sport is awarded mainly on the basis of international success after an athlete has met very stiff standards in her event. An Honorary Master of Sport is a title given for life, for outstanding athletic accomplishments (ie. Olympic medalist).

In 1968 I moved to Leningrad to study in the institute P.F. Lesgafta, one of the best sporting schools in the country. It is here I spent the happiest days of my young adulthood in a very close track and field group. In my relationships with people I learned a great deal here that I was truly thankful for in years to come when I was chosen captain of the USSR women's team. After 1968 a new event appeared – the 100m hurdles. Simultaneously, the 200m hurdles were run and I became a Master of Sport in this event. Unfortunately this event never appeared in international meets to any great extent, so to realize my dream of going to the Olympic Games I would have to run hurdles over 100 metres. Thus my basic sporting speciality was determined.

The turning point in my life was in 1971 when I became a Master of Sport in the 100m hurdles and made the USSR National team which earned me the right to run in the European Championships in Helsinki. I went to Finland with no special hopes and unexpectedly made the final, where I finished 8th and last. What I learned was critical in my development towards becoming an elite hurdler. I took part in a competition with the best and strongest athletes in the world – all the world's best 100m hurdlers are from Europe. All had seemed invincible to me until our meeting on the same track – the famous Karin Balzer (GDR), the powerful Annelie Erhardt (GDR), the determined Teresa Suknevich, and the technician Valerie Bufanu (ROM). The more I rubbed shoulders with them in the same workouts and races, the more often I asked myself: "And how am I worse? Because I can't run as fast as they do." My transformation as an athlete did not occur at the moment, but while running against the best hurdlers, I never felt out of place, I never gave up without a fight and my attitude was one people would remark on as "the battling character of Tatiana Anisimova."

In Helsinki I learned much from fellow team members like Viktor Saneyev, Valeri Borzov and Nadezhda Chizova. All of the young athletes envied the leading masters, their determination, their modesty, their ability to concentrate on the main goal and achieve it. I learned much from them. It is impossible to exaggerate the value of the presence of the older generation as examples and leaders for others to learn from. I learned a great deal in the domain of determination and the ability to devote much more to achieving success by studying their thoughtful approach towards training and their uncompromisingness in both sport and life.

The 1972 Olympics were less than a year away and I was the nation's leading hurdler, but I never got to Munich. At the USSR Nationals in 1972 I repeated my national record of 13.3 in the heats and Lia Khitrina and I ran 13.6 in the final. These results did not match those of foreign athletes, so the selection committee decided to take no hurdlers to Munich. At 22 I was young enough to set my goals for Montreal and still maintain my dream – to make the Olympics.

In 1973 I did not compete. I had a daughter but did not forget my dream. As soon as conditions permitted I began training for the European Championships in Rome in 1974. In the year of my absence from the track my opponents had changed and our strongest hurdler was Natasha Lebedeva. She and I went to the Eternal City. I think I was sent, not for my current results which were not that great, but because I was experienced in such competition. Bestowing this kind of faith in me gave me great strength. I made it to the final where I placed 6th, .01 ahead of Natasha, a time that would divide us at several competitions.

In 1975 my coach became head of his educational faculty and could not devote the necessary time towards training. Therefore I asked one of our best specialist hurdle coaches, the Honourable Master Coach of the USSR, Vyacheslav Sadovsky to become my advisor. This was no ordinary change of coaches, as I had already worked with him on the national team and he knew very well my strengths and weaknesses. My strong side was good speed and rhythm and the development of speed-strength qualities (special strength). My weaknesses were mainly in the area of technique. We decided to devote a fair amount of time to technique in the fine details of preparation for the Montreal Olympics. I ran indoor winter competitions in order not to lose a single day of technique work. This turned out not to be in vain.

Already in May, 1976, I achieved a good result of 12.72 which would have been a national record but was wind aided. I again broke 13.0 seconds at the USSR Championships and won a trip to the Olympics. And so my first dream, now already distant, came true. Could I become the Olympic Champion?

Much has been written about me looking back at the finish. Where did I lose that hundredth of a second that gave the gold medal to Schaller (GDR) (12.77) and the silver (12.78) to me? Looking back was not the cause of my defeat. Those grams of force that I didn't have for the victory had been "run out" in the ill-timed re-run an hour before the final. In my semi-final Lyuba Konanova had fallen and interfered with Valerie Bufanu so the judges had the race re-run. (Ed. note: Bufanu appears in the results under her maiden name of Stefanescu.) It is not without reason that I dislike re-runs now. My mood after Montreal was mixed — happy to have won a medal and sad not to be first.

After the Olympics I began to prepare for the European Championships with my new coach Yuri Ivansovich Anisimov. We worked out a very detailed plan of preparation and competition. Of course I was aiming to win and without any re-runs. But ... at the 1978 European Championships in Prague I once again had to race twice in weather that was both cold and rainy. Even my warm ups demanded a lot of work. Only the desire to get the title (and realize yet another dream) allowed me to carry the run to the finish. But my competitors were younger, had quicker recoveries and once again I came second.

About my participation in the Moscow Olympics I cannot write. Why? Three weeks before the final I raced at 100 metres, resulting in a serious leg injury. I clearly knew I was no longer 20. To the very end I believed my leg would be all right. I went to the start of my heat with my leg bandaged thinking it would help. It didn't. Twice in the heat I felt sharp pains, but I didn't quit and made the semis. It had only become worse and I couldn't run. The next day I left Leningrad and went to the Caspian Sea to rest and forget everything like a nightmare. If only it were a dream ...

I had decided the Olympics would have been my last race if I had won. Since I didn't win, was I to leave the sport with unrealized dreams? So once again I was at the track in the post-Olympic season working out. My training went well with new found energy and strength. This year promised to be successful. This time caution did not leave me for a single second. I could not allow an accidental injury to stand in the way of my dream. It was crucial to plan every detail of my preparation for the main competition of the year – the World Cup in Rome. In 1981 I lost only one race, the USSR Cup in Kiev to an excellently prepared Marina Kemenchezlivi. This did not distress me since I had been tired from stressful dual meets with East Germany, the USA and the European Cup. I simply needed a little rest before the World Cup. Before going to Rome national team members were told that event winners would be given the title of Honoured Master of Sport. I recall the meaningful glance at me at this announcement from the head coach Nikolai Politiko. At this time everyone knew my dream.

In Rome I tried not to think about the outcome of the race. During the warm up rain fell for forty minutes and I had to finish my warm up under the stands in a narrow corridor. There was only one race so everyone would have the same conditions. For the race the track was hidden under a sheet of water and the crowd in the stands was noisy. In the midst of this I could hear the cry, "Go Tania". How I ran I can't recall. I only wanted it to be over fast. When I found out I had won, I couldn't stop the tears. Tears of joy, the joy of realizing a dream.

I am now on the threshold of my 22nd season. This is the season of a new European Championship. I'm often asked if I'll race at my 4th European Championship. Right now I don't know what to answer but I've already started training ...

THE 400 METRE HURDLES: A COLLECTION OF SCIENTIFIC INVESTIGATIONS

Trans. Alan Adamson.
Attributed to Legaya Atletika (USSR), Sept. 82,
which does contain an article on 400m hurdles, but
it does not appear to be this one.

Scientific investigations into 400 metre hurdling are being conducted along several lines: 1) competitive activity; 2) technique; 3) physical preparation; 4) training loads.

Competitive Activity

Examples of the course of hurdle races are presented in the work of the Canadian researcher Brent McFarlane (1980). A basic tendency of improvement of the sporting result among men is connected to the decrease of the number of steps over the distance on account of the fact that more of the hurdles are being reached in 13 strides. So where Dave Hemery in 1968 ran 6 hurdles in 13 strides, and the remaining 4 in 15, then already in Munich in 1972 John Akii-Bua ran 5 in 13, 3 in 14, and only the last 2 in 15. In 1976 in Montreal Edwin Moses ran the whole way with 13 strides between hurdles. The determination of the number of strides between hurdles involves a determination of the stride length. The correspondence between the stride length and the number of strides between hurdles is as follows: for 12 strides — 2.68m, for 13 – 2.45, for 14 – 2.27, for 15 – 2.13, for 16 – 2.00, 17 – 1.85, 18 – 1.64.

Among men there is a tendency to fairly even-paced running over the distance. For example, the variation between the first and second 200 for Hemery was 1.5 seconds, for Akii-Bua 1.8, and for Moses 1.4.

John Akii-Bua has said that to improve Moses' current mark of 47.13, it will be necessary to try to run the race either with fewer strides like him or at a higher speed between hurdles.

The tendencies observed have not yet found use in women's hurdling. The winner of the European Championship of 1978, T. Zelentsova, used the greatest number of strides, running through all the hurdles in 17 strides, while the medallists S. Hollman and K. Rossley over part of the distance used 15 and 16. The variation in time between the first and second 200s varied considerably: for Zelentsova – 1.1 sec., for Hollman – 2.7, and Rossley – 4.0 sec.

Running Technique

Y. Vasiliev (1967) proceeded from the fact that the difficulty of mastering the technique for 400 hurdles consisted of the fact that one must learn to correctly calculate one's motion in the interval between hurdles, and this demands a precise differentiation of distance and of components of technique. Comparative analysis of the running technique of hurdlers at different qualifications shows that the athletes of the highest class are distinguished by their skill directly after touchdown at finding that running rhythm that allows them to precisely calculate the strides to the following barrier. Less qualified athletes, as is known, attempt to adjust their last few strides into a hurdle.

Before going over a hurdle the internal rhythm of running (the relationship between the support phase and flight phase) changes as well. For high class athletes the tempo increases because of a shortened support phase, while for lower level runners on account of a shortened flight phase.

M. Maishutovich has shown that a basic measure determining the growth in mastery of an athlete from the 1st rank to Master of Sport is a decrease of the Rhythmic Coefficient (RC, the ratio of the time of the flight phase to the time of the support phase). It is this author's opinion that the RC is the most objective criterion for evaluating the rhythmic structure of hurdle running. Its decrease reflects the growth of technical mastery of a hurdler. The author demonstrates a high correlation between 400m hurdle results and the RC. The value of the RC for a Master of Sport is established by the author at 0.62-0.65.

E.N. Bulanchik (1975) established that among the best hurdlers in the world the time consumed in going over a hurdle (from takeoff to touchdown) is .35 -.40 seconds. The optimal ratio between the support phase time in the takeoff to the flight time in the hurdling stride is 1.3 to 2, and between support time before the hurdle to support time on the touchdown is 1 to .9. For a decrease in the takeoff time leads to an increased flight time and to a shock on foot plant, and a decrease in the flight time in the last stride but one and an insignificant increase in the support time in the attack on the hurdle is compensated for by a decreased time crossing the hurdle.

In connection with the fact that the women's hurdles are lower than the men's in relation to their height, technique plays a lesser role for women. Some specialists recommend scales of evaluation of the technique of hurdle running based on the difference between 400 metre times on the flat and over hurdles. Since progress in women's 400 hurdles began so recently, one researcher has suggested the following scale: 3.5 sec – excellent technical level; 4-5 sec – good; 5 sec – low level.

Physical Preparedness

Whatever excellent technical habits the hurdler has mastered, he will never get top results unless he runs well on the flat.

The strongest men hurdlers in the world can cover 400 metres in 44.8 – 45.5 seconds. In the 100 they run 10.2 – 10.5. The correlation coefficient between the 400 hurdle times and the 400 and 100 times for the highest qualified runners is roughly .70 (Y. Brogli, P. Christev, 1975) and .77 (M. Dolgii, 1976).

The goal of some work of M. Dolgii (1978) was the study of factors determining the sporting result and the working out on this basis of the most effective means of training for 400 hurdles. The results of a comparative analysis of physical preparedness of hurdlers over 110 and 400 metres, carried out by the author, showed that the physical preparedness of 110 hurdlers at a given level was higher than for 400 hurdlers at the same level. Working from this the author suggests that training for 110 hurdles is a distinctive "school" through which every athlete specializing in 400 hurdles should go. The use of high hurdles should become an integral part of his training, as repeated running over high barriers develops many of the qualities that allow the athlete to quickly and rationally cross the lower hurdles at his basic distance.

Data by M. Dolgii witness the fact that physical qualities play a leading role in the stage of athletic development in 400 hurdles. According to the author this explains the fact that those hurdlers who earlier specialized in 110 hurdles, and passed to the longer race, have greater success than those who have specialized in 400 hurdling from the start.

Other authors also give considerable importance to the development of physical qualities. For example, according to E. Bulanchik (1975), a hurdler with a 13-stride rhythm should have a standing triple jump result of 8.90 – 9.30 metres, and be able to cover over 40 metres in a 13-jump test. Such results can be achieved only by athletes with significant special strength. A.I. Yulin considers (1975) that an athlete with insufficient leg strength should first train a 13-stride rhythm with the hurdles 35m apart.

Specialists considering questions of preparation for 400 metre hurdling remark on the dominant role played by special endurance in the achievement of top results at this distance. A low level of development of special endurance will result in the athlete's being unable to maintain an optimum speed and often leads to "dying" in attempts to cover the distance. On maintaining optimal speed there is also the observation that, according to the Bulgarian investigators I. Brogli and B. Christev, to achieve a 2 second improvement in one's 400 hurdle time requires an improvement in the time from the last hurdle to the finish of .34 sec. but only a .11 sec. improvement in the time between the 1st and 2nd hurdles.

In the view of the well-known Italian coach A. Calvesi, "endurance plus technique are more important things for a 400 hurdler than speed plus technique". He considers that speed of a 400 specialist is not enought for the hurdle event, which has strength requirements not much less than those in an 800.

Many successful 400 hurdlers also race quite well on the flat over longer distances. For example, Dave Hemery achieved excellent indoor performances at 600m. Edwin Moses is considering running 800s with the hope of getting a time near 1:44 while Harald Schmid has run 800 in under 1:45.

Training Loads

Hurdle running is a technically complicated track exercise and therefore improving the technique of hurdle clearance is one of the major aims of training. While developing whatever physical qualities, one must simultaneously train to clear hurdles and master the rhythm of running between them.

Bulanchik's investigations revealed the difference between the running action of sprinters and of hurdlers running between hurdles and does not recommend that the hurdler devote himself excessively to sprint training. He believes this levels out the special qualities needed in hurdling and leads the hurdler to develop a style close to that of the sprinter. He advises 400 hurdlers in the winter preparatory period to run over 1-3 hurdles at submaximal and maximal speeds, with repetitions of this from 4 to 10 times, and in the summer period to cover 1-7 hurdles with 4 to 7 reps. In the winter period with the goal of perfecting technique of hurdle clearance and maintaining the necessary stride length (to maintain 13-14 strides between hurdles) he recommends the inclusion in training of clearing 3-4 hurdles at a height of 100cm set about 15-15.5 m. apart, and taking 5-6 strides between.

To increase the athlete's ability to run the distance at the necessary rhythm, the author believes that special running exercises, such as running a flat 400 at the hurdle running rhythm, running under one's own momentum after reaching top speed (with the goal of increasing stride length), 5-13-jumps from leg to leg.

Analyzing the weekly cycles of some of the leading runners in the world and in our country, Bulanchik reveals some distinctions in the planning and distribution of means of training. The majority of the strongest athletes in the world aim to increase their speed work at the end of the week or to race. As for our hurdlers, their weeks seem to end with some distance running or some sporting game.

M. Dolgii recommends in the preparatory period more attention on the short hurdle distance, than on the increase of flat 400 running speed. According to his data, a .1 second improvement in 110 hurdle time makes possible a 400 hurdle improvement of .18 seconds, while a .1 second improvement in the flat 400 yields only a .06 second improvement over hurdles.

M. Maishutvich has shown that parallel development of endurance and mastery of hurdles rhythm (running with 10m intervals between hurdles in the preparatory period) will be the most optimal correspondence of running to hurdle preparation for qualified 400 hurdlers. For highly-ranked hurdlers the most optimal is a variant of training in which 60% of the work is devoted to hurdle preparation and 40% to running. The breakdown of running in the preparatory period is about 20% intervals from 30 to 300m and 80% intervals from 400 to 600m.

Many specialists in hurdling agree that it is necessary to base training on the rhythm that is to be used in racing. Y. M. Lituey (1976) argues that to race with a 13-stride rhythm, one must prepare for this in the preparatory period.

As for the training of women 400 hurdlers, O. Stashny (1978) considers that one should orient oneself on the basis of the experience with men.

LEVEL OF ASPIRATION OF SUPERIOR ATHLETES

By Brent McFarlane. See Bibliography Item 49.

What distinguishes the successful athlete from the unsuccessful? What is that stoic, gutty drive within the human mind that pushes an athlete to the extremes of pain, both physically and mentally, for that minute moment of time we call success? What role does motivation, and one's *level of aspiration*, play in successful running? To become a great athlete, one must have an intense and persisting urge to do so.

The purpose of this article is, first, from the material available to give a definition of the level of aspiration (LA); second, to discuss the research done in this field; third, to examine relative applications to performance; and fourth, to give the coach an understanding of how to increase athletic performance levels.

The concept of motivation is an important one when considering any type of human behaviour. Motivation is simply "the general level of arousal to action or urge to push toward a specific goal"[3]. In order to consider the process of motivating an athlete, it is necessary to specifically limit the issues at hand. First, external or extrinsic motivation is caused by some artificial outside reason which normally does not arise from itself[3]. Second, internal or intrinsic motivation arises from some inner cause, drive, wish, or need that requires no external reason[3]. Each athlete is personally responsible for providing his own internal motivation. That immeasurable factor, which some call "spirit" or "guts", is often the determining factor in many races. Nothing can compensate for the lack of will to fight when the situation demands. Only the individual athlete can provide his own personal, internal motivation. In every race there may be more than one moment when the body wants to quit. It needs internal motivation to survive the crisis. Otherwise, the penalty is defeat. The difference between a winner and a loser is often trying. The winner tries. There is no failure like ceasing to try.

In searching to understand internal motivation, one of the basic underlying factors is one's level of aspiration. In attaining what R. Frost calls "peak performances" in sports[27], he quotes from Bob Richards in 'The Heart of a Champion': "If you're going to be great in sports you've got to have something else ... I've been amazed to see mediocre athletes, fellows drifting along with great potential but never really realizing their full abilities, suddenly inspired...they would do the impossible. In a matter of a few months they would become sensations and people would wonder what had happened. I'd like to give you one facet of what I think it means when a person is inspired. It's when they see themselves not as they are but as they can become. It's when they see themselves, not in terms of their weaknesses and shortcomings, their failures and inadequacies, but in terms of what they can be, when they begin to believe they can be what their vision tells them. That's when they're inspired, when they no longer see their weaknesses, but their greatnesses; by emphasizing their strengths they go on to do things they never dreamed of."

This level of awareness of incentive to perform better in future performances is what is termed Level of Aspiration (LA). This energy is present in each of us – physical and mental – not at one level or another, but within a range of possible use and development. This range is both broad and flexible. Its upper limits are far beyond what seem humanly possible and healthful, if one considers the limited demands for human energy. Further, those who reach the upper levels of this range can be active day after day, year after year with no ill effects to health or longevity. Their organisms and mind develop, not only resulting in superior performances, and consequently the releasing of physiological reserves of energy, but also an increase in their LA.

Affiliation, the need to join a set of people, is related to one's self-evaluation to obtain acceptance. An individual's LA is related to his perceived order or standing in a group with whom the athlete feels some close attachments. This is related to one's maturity. Allport[1] found that children are more susceptible to social implications of a task than are adults, because the greater amount of past experience, in the case of adults, stabilizes their estimate about future performances more than the case with the less-mature individual. As a man matures, his needs for social affiliation decreased, while he developed a high level of self esteem and aspiration in the individual sport of running, where the glory and recognition went to himself, not the group. Also with maturity came experience, and with this success developed and his LA increased.

Another factor closely related to achievement of goals and LA is the nature and amount of past experience in the task. Cratty[15] states that past experiences provide a "perceptual anchoring point" upon which to base estimates of subsequent performances, and the amount and quality of the past experience or knowledge of past performance scores and its relationship to the task at hand, influences both the accuracy of self-estimation and the difference between estimation and actual performance achieved.

This is known as "goal discrepancy" – the difference between LA and level of performance. A positive goal discrepancy, or D score, represents an LA which is higher than the previous performance. Also, an attainment discrepancy score is the difference between LA and the level of subsequent performances. An athlete is considered to have succeeded if the level of subsequent performance surpassed the LA set. It may be said that the level of aspiration presupposes a goal, which has an inner structure consisting of an ideal goal and an action goal. The ideal goal is the ultimate goal the individual hopes to attain sometime in the future. The action goal is the momentary goal the individual tries for because of the present unobtainability of the ideal goal. LA is usually considered to be the action goal.

Frank[26] states that the LA is influenced by the relative strengths of three needs: the need to make LA approximate the level of future performance as closely as possible, the need to keep the LA as high as possible regardless of past performances and the need to avoid failure. The more an athlete punches through the fatigue barrier and the pain barrier, to that area of the third and fourth wind, the more aware he became of his potentialities. He underwent arduous work one day so that the next day he could do the same work load more easily and enjoyably at a higher level.

Success is progress towards a worthwhile goal. Definite and realistic goals must be set. Since LA can be defined as "the goal, expectation, or self-demands which an individual associates with a performance of a specific task", it is imperative that a man's goals should not exceed his grasp. Robinson[100] and Atkinson[5] found that highly-motivated individuals, those with a high need for achieve-

230

ment, set moderate, realistic goals. Conversely, those who possessed high fear of failure often set goals so low they could not fail, or so high that success was highly unlikely. Very hard or very easy tasks cause no sense of success of failure and likely are protecting the athlete from feelings of failure. Failing to reach an impossible goal could not be subjectively considered a failure. By choosing a realistic goal, these individuals would expose themselves to the risk of failure. It is impractical, if not impossible, to comprehend the innumerable cross-currents of racial inheritance, social traditions, institutional demands, family expectations, friendly encouragements, aggressions, impulsions, insecurities, frustrations and goals that can and do motivate athletes to run. When athletes first begin to run, their motives and goals are probably as low in order as their performances: to win a medal, to make the team or be one of the group. First established were a set of short-ranged goals which were attainable, which gradually and progressively led to long range goals, i.e. the Olympics.

It should be pointed out at this time that temporary defeat may not lower the LA. With repeated success, an occasional defeat could act to release pressure or be brushed off as a bad day. However, generally most individuals follow what Heckhausen[30] calls "The Laws of Shifting" -individuals will raise LA after success and lower it after failure. Temporary defeat or setbacks can often be valuable teachers. Festinger[22] found that there was tendency after failure to lower LA.

Once a firm goal is planted in an athlete's mind, he is on his way to success, because he knows where he's going. The attainment of success is half-accomplished when an athlete directs his thoughts towards succeeding at a goal. He must also think of the means of achieving his goal, the effort, toil and work. An athlete becomes what he plants in his mind. Planting the goal of success in his mind is one of the athlete's most important personal responsibilities in achieving success. It is this necessary seed, "fertilized" by hard work and goal directed behaviour, from which the LA blooms. Success is associated with winning, which both in turn are dependent on LA. Cratty[5] states that the final shaping of performance is primarily dependent upon LA, which in turn molds the intensity of the effort expanded. The following diagram will explain further. Feedback (to be discussed later) of success or failure may affect the motives by shifting, depending on the performance levels.

Physiological Factors
Structural Factors
Psychological Factors
Social Factors
Social-Cultural-Economic Factors
Background of Athlete
Aspiration Level Prior
to Competition

Feedback   Feedback

Performance in Competition

Performance Goal

Interpretation of
Success or Failure

To discuss success extensively, reference will be made to a paper by D. Hunter, "Level of Aspiration."[33] The concept of LA, while not simple, can be and has been one of the underlying criteria for success. To repeat, success is founded on the principle that human beings become the end product of their thoughts – they believe and succeed. The construct "subjective probability of success (SP_{su})" is useful in explaining the initial setting of LA and shifts in the level after success or failure. The Valence (Vn) of any level of difficulty is influenced by the SP_{su} associated with the choice taken – ranging from 0 to 100 percent with a high probability of success denoting an easy task. For example, an SP_{su} of .90 would be attached to an easy task, while a task with an SP_{su} of .50 is one which the individual feels he has an equal chance of success or failure. It is assumed that the SP_{su} plus the subjective probability of failure (SP_F) equals unity. A choice with an SP_{su} of .70 would therefore have a SP_F of .30. This would occur in a race situation where there are only one or two top competitors entered instead of a whole field of international runners, where his SP_F may be lower – depending on his LA. In many races an athlete's SP_{su} is not against other runners in the race, but against a record or personal best, therefore being .50.

To further explain the idea of success, Deutsch and Kraus[16] stated that SP_{su} was influenced by past experience in the task. This is especially true related to the latest performance of the task.

The valence of the level of difficulty then becomes:

$$Vn = (Va\ Suc.\ Sp_{su}) - (Va\ Fai.Sp_F)$$
$$Va\ Suc = valence\ of\ success$$
$$Va\ Fai = valence\ of\ failure$$

The LA is taken as the level of difficulty that has the highest possible valence. The initial LA set by an elite athlete would have an SP_{su} of .50 because the valence of this choice would be, at a maximum, related to his strong achievement motive. If he succeeded then the SP_{su} associated with the task would rise and he would choose a more difficult level with a SP_{su} of .50 attached to it, in his case meet records, or world records, or defeating the best competition available. Athletes with a strong motive to avoid failure would select either high or low SP_{su}.

What effect did defeat have on an athlete? Defeat may be difficult to survive and at the same time maintain a high LA in performance. Defeat may be a punishment to an athlete if he was intensely aroused to run and battle his hardest only to lose. How much of such punishment he can endure depends on his previous success. It is up to the athlete and coach to determine how much of this stimulus (in this case defeat) the athlete can endure without becoming overtense, overexcited and upset in performance. The effects of failure on the LA are far more varied than those of success. When an individual experiences a performance below his LA, he may see it as a threat to his self-esteem or ego; therefore he may keep his LA low to prevent such situations from arising a second time or too high so it is impossible to reach, thus no one can blame him for failing.

The question may be logically asked, "Does correct training guarantee success and a consequent raise in one's LA?" The answer is no, but it does make competitive success possible, providing other factors such as physical capacity and ability are present. Such mental factors as courage, competitive instinct, will-to-win, subconscious desire for victory, capacity to suffer, ability to ignore pain, perserverence, tenacity, frustration tolerance, and "guts", combine with correct training to transform competitive potential into a reality, giving assurance of success and a raise in LA.

Roger Bannister, the first man to run a mile under four minutes, wrote: "For 10 years I have been running many times a week and my grasp of the reasons why I continue to run grow. Running through mud and rain is never boring. I find in running a deep satisfaction that I cannot express – win or lose. However strenuous our work, sports brings more pleasure than some easier relaxations. It brings joy, freedom and challenge which cannot be found elsewhere... I sometimes think running has given me a glimpse of the greatest feeling man can know – the simultaneous liberation of both body and mind."[6] Running is as much an affair of the heart as the brain. The point is, both the heart and the brain are needed for successful running. The LA is dependent upon both of these variables. Without the heart, there would be no desire to get there; without the brain, there would be no knowing how to get there.

In all of this striving to achieve a goal, stress can affect the LA. Mental stress is initiated by the nerve centers of the hypothalamus which influence the anterior pituitary gland to secrete the hormone ACTH, which in turn is transported through the blood stream and stimulates glandular activity in the adrenal cortex. The fact that emotional upset can affect the body – physiologically and mentally – suggests strongly that being psychologically well-adjusted, emotionally stable, happy and successful, would remove undue stress. The stress of training and racing is primarily a mental-emotional problem, not a physical one. Fundamentally, racing is not a struggle against one's opponents, but rather against oneself. Opponents help. One's program of training must be very effective in reducing stress; however the key to developing a high LA is dependent upon relaxation. Relaxation is achieved by gradually losing one's self-awareness, especially of negative aspects of effect and fatigue (physical and mental). This may happen best and most completely by accepting things for what they are, without doubt or fear. Relaxation in running is related to one's approach to life in general. It develops more from unconscious than conscious learning, out of experiencing with composure the pain of training and anguish of early defeat. All great runners accept discomforts and disappointments as part of running. Through year-round training under all conditions the champion becomes inured to suffering. Good training hurts, for every new level of development or intensity of effort brings its own quality of pain. To deliberately choose the difficult path in training tends to produce greater running powers and raises one's probability of success – one basis for a higher LA. Practice, physically and mentally, helps to remove and master stress.

Finally, the role the coach plays on the LA – perhaps the most dominant underlying factor influencing the athlete – must be considered. A coach must keep in mind that each athlete is an individual having different motives or goals, and therefore, must appeal to the athlete on his own milieu. He should carefully assist the athlete in identifying his goals, both short and long-range. Goals should be realistic, measurable, progressively higher and attainable. The success of failure of goal attainment has a direct influence on the LA as stated in the Laws of Shifting[30].

Second, identification of significant obstacles which impede or prevent goal attainment is of utmost importance. Recognizing and admitting the actual barriers to success on a personal basis is often impossible for the athlete himself. The coach is in a unique position to pinpoint impediments to goal-attainment and assist in the organization of action and formulation of plans to overcome these obstacles, i.e. problems in training, competition attitude, tactical judgment, health, home environment and educational environment. All athletes are faced with the ever-present problem of acquiring more and more strength, aerobic and anaerobic endurance, power, and speed. Most of these are developed through training. To succeed there will always be obstacles.

Perhaps the most important role of the coach is that of "information feedback". *Instrinsic* or *kinesthetic information* arises within the body and represents a pooling of kinesthetic and perceptual cues that are natural consequences of movement.

Extrinsic feedback arises from artificial cues from the environment such as the coach. Feedback is the strongest, most important variable which controls performance, success and learning. If behaviour is goal-directed then the successful approach to the goal – indicated by feedback – can serve to sustain a high LA. The coach has the power to "mold" an athlete. He cannot control the athlete's LA but he can influence extrinsic feedback in the form of motivators. The coach functions to focus the athlete's attention on improving the quality of desirable elements already present in his performance and add missing elements. Cratty[15] found that feedback in the form of instruction is more effective if presented in positive terms – what to do – rather than negative – what not to do. Coaching suggestions should be concrete and specific. This requires less rigid, less formal and a more individualized coaching method. A program must be very effective in giving positive feedback in terms of goal-selection, obstacle-identification, action-planning, technical knowledge, enthusiasm, personality, self-confidence, character, aggressiveness, morals, and other assets desirable in successful coaching. The effect on the LA is very significant in which continuous external and internal feedback resulted in a high LA.

In most races there comes a crucial point where victory hangs in the balance. At that instant, no matter how cleverly an athlete has been coached, the issue of victory or defeat passed entirely to him. Only then did his powers of physical and mental courage, willpower, and guts stand exposed. Only internal motivation directly underlied by a high LA could provide this answer when faced with this moment of truth.

In conclusion, much care must be taken by the coach to create character and pride within the athlete himself, not only for superior performance but also particular to individual development. Through extrinsic motivation one is able to coach and train a human being in the physical aspect of life, but also of equal importance is the ability to create a unique mind with an aspiration level. Any athlete thinks, feels, plans and executes what he does with such great success. Motivated – yes! High level of aspiration – yes! But above all a unique athlete who has set his goals, attacked them, and succeeded in conquering them.

THE AUTOGENIC WAY

By Brent McFarlane. See Bibliography Item 82.

"The entire East German team was lying in a field in the Olympic Village doing an autogenic training session. The concept of total relaxation and control has been very positive in assisting athletic performance. This is a science that many world class athletes are developing to its maximum."

Esko Olkonen. National Coach, Finland

Concentration, relaxation and control are the secrets of many personal bests. Increased concentration is the result of training. Autogenic training is concentrative self-relaxation.

There are many demands made upon an athlete's self-control and ability to concentrate including tenseness at the beginning of an event, negative expectations, a fear of failure or of success, inability to relax, distractions before and during a competition, over-stimulation and lack of motivation. These problems and many others are a serious threat to success in a competitive situation.

Language can communicate feelings to the brain which controls the body, appropriately structured language can dramatically affect bodily changes. Autogenic training utilizes this system to strengthen neural pathways. Athletes can learn to develop appropriate mental strategies to regulate the signals to the brain, and gain control over the body's physiological functions. Learning to control blood pressure, pulse, level of arousal, muscular tension and competitive pressure enhances the athlete's ability to perform.

Autogenic training can prevent the neural-muscular system from going off track but, anyone who has difficulty concentrating will have trouble learning the technique. Injuries are often a result of tenseness which can be reduced with the effective use of autogenic training. Athletes must practice in their minds (as do musicians). The body must be trained to respond to verbal cues. Difficult sequences of motion can be improved to the point of perfection by concentration.

Mental relaxation and confidence may be as effective as physical training. Positive attitudes and expectations will lead to that "winning feeling".

Consider the following session of basic autogenic training, as outlined by J.L. Mason in his book "Guide to Stress Reduction". Get yourself into a comfortable position (lying) and close your eyes. Take a deep, slow breath and pause. Repeat several times. Allow yourself to feel heavy and warm. Say to yourself. "I am at peace with myself and fully relaxed." (repeat 6 times). Breathe naturally and slowly. Exhale completely. Try feeling the heaviness in your arms and say, "My right arm is heavy." (repeat 6 times). Allow yourself to let go of the muscles in your arm: "My left arm is heavy." (repeat 6 times). Then do your legs, repeating the phrase 6 times for each leg and your neck and shoulders.

As you breathe slowly repeat the following sequence (6 times each) "My right arm is warm – my left arm is warm. My neck and shoulders are warm." Follow with, "My heartbeat is calm and regular – my breathing is calm and regular – my abdominal region is warm and calm – my forehead is cool and smooth."

Breathe slowly and naturally, allowing yourself to breathe away tension. Let your thoughts rise up and out of your consciousness, let them drift away. Your mind will gradually become calm and clear as you let go of distractions and drift deeper into relaxation. Imagine you are at the top of a slowly moving escalator and as you step on you find yourself gradually riding down deeper and deeper into relaxation. Drift slowly into a comfortable spot and allow yourself to lie down, just sinking into the warm earth. Feel the warm of the sunlight and a warm breeze warms your legs and feet. Let the warmth spread to every part of the body. Drift deeper and deeper into peace. Register this calmness in your mind. Stay in this state for a few minutes.

Everytime you practice this sequence you will be able to relax more and more. The will to control tension increases as feelings of calmness and relaxation replace them.

Gently bring yourself up from deep relaxation to a more alert state, gradually let yourself become more aware of your surroundings but remain calm and relaxed. Repeat 6 times, "I am fresh and alert." The basic session ends here. Sessions related specifically to an event, or tension related to that event, are not done in early sessions.

Visualization is a skill that improves with practice. Warmth and heaviness are easier to feel for some than others. Letting go and clearing the mind of distractions will come with time. Not wanting to come out of the state of deep relaxation is normal, but once you have mastered the technique, you can recall the peaceful, calm feeling throughout the rest of the day or competition.

A possible 12 week training program (5 days a week) would consider the following elements:

Week 1-2:	muscular relaxation
Week 3-4:	mental relaxation
Week 5:	supplementary training
Week 6:	dissociation and detachment training
Week 7:	goal programming training
Week 8:	ideo-motor training
Week 9:	problem solving
Week 10:	problem solving
Week 11:	assertive training
Week 12:	concentration training

For further reading, see Bibliography Items 39, 44, 46, and 103.

APPENDIX C

Test your knowledge

"Now you try it!"

APPENDIX C

TEST YOUR KNOWLEDGE

The following section is designed to allow the coach to test his knowledge from the contents of the book. As part of the CTFA National Certification Program an examination will follow all courses. Some of the questions listed will appear on this exam. You are asked to work individually or in groups to be able to present the answers to selected questions.

1) Explain diagramatically your coaching position, listing the 10 most important features you would consider during a 400m hurdle race.

2) The body lean of a woman hurdler in the 100m hurdles is essentially different from that of the men's 110m hurdles. Explain.

3) Describe a technically competent high hurdle clearance from take-off to landing with specific reference to the mechanical principles involved.

4) Give an analysis of the factors which influence the positioning and spacing of the starting blocks for one of the hurdle races.

5) Do a film analysis of a Canadian hurdler using the condensed diagnostic sheet provided. State positive and negative biomechanical observations.

HURDLING DIAGNOSTIC SHEET

Name _____ Date of Evaluation _____ Coach _____

Front	Side

1. Sprinting Technique
   (i)   Drive phase
   (ii) Recovery phase
   (iii) Skill development

2. Start and Approach
   (i) Starting technique
   (ii) Approach to H 1

3. Take Off
   Action at the Hurdle
   (i)   Lead leg
   (ii) Trail leg
   (iii) Arms and shoulders
   (iv) Total take-off action

4. Clearance
   Over the Hurdle
   (i) Lead leg
   (ii) Trail leg
   (iii) Total picture

5. Landing
   Action from the Hurdle
   (i) Lead leg
   (ii) Trail leg
   (iii) Total picture

6. Total Hurdle Race
   (i) Action between H 1-5
   (ii) Action between H 5-10
   (iii) Last hurdle to finish

6) Using the appropriate energy systems, design a training programme for an athlete whom you have coached over the past year. Give name, age, event and best performances. Include yearly programme of phases, macrocycles, microcycles and a sample of a weekly programme for the athlete for each phase.

7) Discuss stride pattern, touchdown times, differentials and race rehearsing drills for a male 52.00 400m hurdler. Use the following diagram to illustrate your answer.

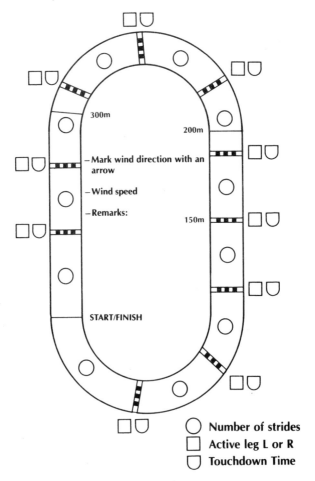

- Mark wind direction with an arrow
- Wind speed
- Remarks:

○ Number of strides
□ Active leg L or R
⊍ Touchdown Time

8) Design a programme for a 14.0 100m female hurdler showing sample workouts for each of the 6 phases of preparation. Include macro- and microcycles with individual sessions and units.

9) Explain diagramatically your coaching angles, listing 10 important features you would consider during a hurdle clearance. State the hurdle event you are discussing and the mechanical principles you are considering.

10) "I win my race to the first hurdle" is stated by many world class hurdlers. Discuss the importance and approach to the 1st hurdle in the 100m or 110m hurdles with specific reference to selecting a correct block position.

11) Design workouts to perfect the last three hurdles in the women's 100m hurdle race.

12) Design workouts to rehearse hurdles 4, 5 and 6 in the men's 400m hurdles.

13) Discuss the factors and design a strength programme for a 110m hurdler running 14.80.

14) Look at a yearly programme in terms of placement of regeneration. Detail the regeneration patterns you would use.

15) Identify one key hurdling injury and design a rehabilation programme.

BIBLIOGRAPHY

With gratitude and a sincere thank you I wish to acknowledge the following world authorities and personal friends.

Calvesi, Alessandro. (Italy). Former National and Olympic Hurdle Coach; Professor at Brescia University.

Dick, Frank. (Great Britain). Director of Coaching, British
Amateur Athletics Board; National and Olympic
Coach.

Dostal, Emil. (Czechoslovakia). Professor, Sports Institute
Prague.

Ewen, Sandy, (Scotland). Staff Coach.

Folkman, S. (Denmark). National and Olympic Hurdle
Coach.

Francis, Charlie. (Canada). National and Olympic Sprint
Coach.

Houston, Mike. (Canada). Professor, University of Waterloo (Ontario).

Mach, Gerard. (Canada). National Program Director
(CTFA); former National and Olympic Coach (Poland
and Canada).

Stephan, Dr. Hervé.(France). Professor, Sports Institute
Paris; Olympic Coach.

Olkonen, Esko. (Finland). Former National and Olympic
Hurdle Coach.

Reid, Pat. (Canada). National and Olympic High Jump
Coach.

Wilt, Fred. (USA). Former editor Track Technique; Track
Coach, Purdue University.

1   Allport, F., "*Influence of Group upon Association and Thought*", *Journal of Experimental Psychology*, 3, 1920, pp. 159-182.

2   Anonymous, "The Modern Training System-Your System", *Yessis Review*, 10, 1975, pp. 57-61.

3   Armstrong, N., "Muscle Power:Food for Sport", *Athletic Coach*, London: British Amateur Athletic Board, December, 1980.

4   Astrand, P.O., and Rodahl, K., *Textbook of Work Physiology*, New York: McGraw Hill Book Co., 1970.

5   Atkinson, J.W., *An Introduction to Motivation*, N.Y.: Van Nostrand, 1964.

6   Bannister, R., *The First Four Minutes*, London Press, 1955.

7   Bilodeau, E.A. & Bilodeau, J. "Motor Skills Learning", *Annual Review of Psychology*, 42, 1961, pp. 243-280.

8   Boas, J., and Osborne, N. "Periodization for Australian Athletes", *Modern Athlete and Coach*, (Australia), April, 1981.

9   Bompa, T., *Theory and Methodology of Training*, Dubuque: Kendal/Hunt, 1983.

10   Bompa, T., and Denis, R., Coach Training Diary, Ottawa: Coaching Association of Canada, 1986.

12   Bosen, K. and Wilt, F. *Motivation and Coaching Psychology*, Los Altos, CA: Tafnews Press, 1971.

13   Breiser, V.,"Hurdling Phases", *Legaya Atletika*, Moscow, 1978. Translated in *Modern Athlete and Coach*, (Australia), July 1979, pp. 5-6.

14   Chu, Don and Vermeil, Al. *Speed, Strength, Power*, Creative Sports Technology Inc., USA, 1982.

15   Cratty, B.J., *Social Dimensions of Physical Activity*, Englewood Cliffs, N. Jersey: Prentice-Hall, 1967.

16   Deutsch, M., and Kraus, R.M. *Thoeries in Social Psychology*, NY, Basic Books Inc. 1965.

17   Dick, F., "Periodization: An Approach to the Training Year", *Track Technique*, (USA), 62, 1975, pp. 1968-1969.

18   Dick, F. *Training Theory*, London: British Amateur Athletic Board, 1978 (reprinted 1984).

19   Dick, F. *Sports Training Principles*, London: Lepus Books, 1980.

20   Doherty, J.K., *Track and Field Omnibook*, Pennsylvania: Swarthmore Publications, 1972. (4th ed. Los Altos, CA: Tafnews Press, 1985).

21   Dyson, G.H., *The Mechanics of Athletics*, London, University of London Press, 1962, (7th ed. London, Sydney, Auckland and Toronto: Hodder & Stoughton: 1977).

22   Festinger, L., "Wish, Expectation, and Group Standards as Factors Influencing LA", *Journal of Abnormal and Social Psychology*, 37, 1942, 184-200.

23   Fitts, P.M. and Posner, M. *Human Performance*, Belmont CA: Brooks-Cole, 1967.

24   Folkman, S., *Haekklob*, Dansk Athletic Forbund, 1980, (revised 1982).

25   Fritsche, G., "Leg Power Exercises for Young Athletes", *Der Leichtathlet*, (German Democratic Republic), November, 1976.

26 Frank, J.D., "Individual Difference in Certain Aspects of LA", *American Journal of Psychology*, 47, 1957, pp. 111-128.

27 Frost, R., *Psychological Concepts Applied to Physical Education and Coaching*, Reading, Mass: Addison-Wesley, 1971.

28 Gambetta, V., "Hurdling and Steeplechasing", Booklet of the Month, No. 38, *Runners World* (USA), August 1975.

29 Godik, M., "The Preparatory Period", *Yessis Review* (USA), 11, December, 1976, pp. 85-88.

30 Heckhausen, H., *The Anatomy of Achieving Motivation*, NY: Academic Press, 1967.

31 Hoppe, F., "Erfolg and Misserfolg", *Psychologie Forschung*, Germany, 14, 1930, pp. 1-62.

32 Houston, M.E., "Metabolic Responses to Exercise, With Special Reference to Training and Competition in Swimming", *Swimming Medicine IV*, Univ. Park Press, 1978.

33 Hunter, D. *Level of Aspiration* (paper), University of Alberta, 1971.

34 Jarver, Jess, ed. *The Hurdles: Contemporary Theory, Technique and Training*, Los Altos, CA: Tafnews Press, 1981. This book is a collection of articles on hurdling reprinted with permission or adapted by the authors from other works. Included are four contributions by Brent McFarlane. See pp. 5-6 for sources.

35 Johnson, C., "Strength Foundations", *Athletic Coach* (England), vol. 10, no. 4, December, 1976.

36 Jordan, P. and Spencer, B. *Champions in the Making*, Eaglewood Cliffs, N. Jersey: Prentice-Hall, 1968.

37   King, W. and Gollnock, P. "Energy Release in the Muscle Cell", *Medicine and Science in Sports*, vol 1, March 1969.

38   Klavora, Boris, "Planning the Training Schedule", Ottawa: *Coaching Association of Canada*, pk 7, item 3.

39   Klavora, P., *Coach. Athlete and the Sport Psychologist*, Univ. of Toronto Press, 1979.

40   Kruger, A., "Periodization, or Peaking at the Right Time", *Track Technique*, (USA), 54, 1973, pp. 1720-24.

41   Lawther, J.D., *Psychology of Coaching*, Englewood Cliffs, N. Jersey: Prentice-Hall, 1968.

42   LeMasurier, J., *Hurdling*, 3rd. ed. London: British Amateur Athletic Board, 1972.

43   Lezchenko, A., *Specialized Strength Training for Sprinters*, 1982 (translated in *Soviet Sports Review* (USA), vol. 18, no. 1, March 1983.

44   Lindemann, H., *Relieve Tension the Autogenic Way*, NY: Peter H. Wyden Inc., 1980.

45   Mach, G., *Sprints, Hurdles, Relays*, Ottawa: Canadian Track & Field Association, 1975.

46   Mason, J.L., *Guide to Stress Reduction*, Culver City, CA: Peace Press Co., 1980.

47   Matveyev, L.P., *Periodisierung des sportlichen Trainings*, Berlin: Verlag Bartels & Wernitz, Frankfurt, 1972.

48   McInnis, A., "A Research Review of Systemized Approaches to Planned Performance Peaking with Relation to the Sport of Track and Field", *Track and Field Journal* (Canada), no. 7, Feb, 1981, pp. 12-16.

McFarlane, A. Brent. (Publications and articles are listed by year.)

1972

[49] "Level of Aspiration of Superior Athletes", *Track Technique*, (USA), 50, December, pp. 1578-1583.

1977

[50] "Touchdown Times for Hurdles", *Track Technique* (USA), March, no. 67, pp.2128-2129. (See also notes to entry no. 57.)

[51] "Creativity in Middle Distance – Something New and Old", *United States Track and Field Quarterly*, vol. 77, no. 4, pp. 47-50.

1978 [52] "Touchdown Charts", *Athletica* (Canada), vol. 5, no. 2, March-April, 1978, p.18.

[53] "Strength Specificity-What is it?", *OTFA Technical Bulletin* (Canada), vol. VI, no. 1, Winter, pp. 22-27. Reprinted in Athletic Coach (England), December pp. 6-10 and (as "Strength Specificity for Sprinters and Hurdlers") in United States Track and Field Quarterly, vol. 80, no. 2 Summer, 1980, pp. 59-61.

[54] "The Women's 400m Hurdles", *OTFA Technical Bulletin* (Canada), vol. VI, no. 2, Spring, pp.33-38.

[55] "Touchdown Charts", *Atletika* (Czechoslovakia), April.

[56] "The Women's 400m Hurdles", *Athletic Coach* (England), September, pp.2-9.

[57] "Touchdown Times", *United States Track and Field Quarterly*, vol. 78, no. 4, p. 33. Reprinted as "Touchdown Times for Hurdlers" in Athletics Coach (Gt. Britain), December, 1979, pp. 31-32. These articles are substantially the same as No. 50, which has a few extra comments.

58   "Hurdle Exercises – Compulsory and Daily", *United States Track & Field Quarterly*, vol. 78, no. 4, pp.36-37.

1979

59   "Hurdling Diagnostic Sheet", *OTFA Technical Bulletin* (Canada), Summer, no. 27, pp.1-6.

60   "Jumping Exercises", *OTFA Technical Bulletin* (Canada), Fall, no. 28, pp. 16-20.

61   "Skill Preparation", *Athletic Coach* (Gt. Britain), June, pp. 28-30.

62   "Warm up and Flexibility Exercises", *Athletic Coach* (Gt. Britain), September, pp. 19-22.

63   "Even pacing for 800 Metres", *United States Track & Field Quarterly*, vol. 79, no. 3, pp. 43-46.

1980

64   "Hurdling Diagnostic Sheet, *United States Track & Field Quarterly*, vol. 80, no. 2, Summer, pp. 54-55.

65   "Understanding the 400m Hurdles", *United States Track & Field Quarterly*, vol. 80, no. 2, Summer, pp. 56-68. Reprinted in *Track and Field Journal* (Canada), October no. 5, pp. 9-10 and in *OTFA Technical Bulletin* (Canada), no. 32, Fall, pp. 7-10. The USTFQ article has three extra charts not contained in the reprints.

66   "Rhythm for 100m Hurdles", *Athletic Coach* (England), June, pp. 14-15.

67   "Warm up and Flexibility Exercises", *OTFA Technical Bulletin* (Canada), Spring, pp. 21-24.

68   "Hills-A Variety of Uses", *Athletic Coach* (England), September, pp. 8-9. Also in *United States Track & Field Quarterly*, Fall, vol. 80, no. 3.

69   "Rhythm – A Quest for Speed", *Track and Field Journal* (Canada), October, no. 5, pp. 9-10.

70   "Hurdling", *Newfoundland and Labrador T&F Quarterly* (Canada).

71   "Flexibility for Sprinters and Hurdlers", *Modern Athlete and Coach* (Australia), October, pp. 35-37.

72   "Calvesi", *Ontario Athletics* (Canada) December-January, pp.14-15. Reprinted as "Calvesi-An Artist" in *Track Technique* (USA), 83, Spring 1981, pp. 2637-2638. A shortened version is also printed in *United States Track and Field Quarterly*, vol. 81, no. 2, Summer pp. 51-52.

73   "Understanding the 110m High Hurdles", *OTFA Technical Bulletin* (Canada), no. 32, Fall, pp. 1-6. Reprinted with minor changes in *Modern Athlete and Coach* (USA), January 1981, pp. 7-9. The *OTFA Technical Bulletin* article has extra diagrams and a reference list.

74   "Simple Hurdle Evaluation", *OTFA Technical Bulletin* (Canada), no. 32, Fall, pp. 19-21.

75   "Rhythm – The Key to Hurdling", *Track Technique* (USA), 81, Fall, pp. 2569-2570.

1981
76   "Sprint-Hurdle Skill Development", *Track Technique* (USA), 82, Winter, pp. 2605-2606.

77   "XI European Coaches Congress Report", *Ontario Athletics* (Canada), August, pp. 14-15. Reprinted, with the deletion of two paragraphs, in *Track and Field Journal* (Canada), no. 17, October, pp. 12-13.

78   "Specific Starting Exercises", *Modern Athlete and Coach* (Australia), July, pp. 36-38. Reprinted with minor changes in *Track Technique Annual 1981* (USA), Fall and in *OTFA Technical Bulletin* (Canada), no. 36, Fall, pp. 10-12.

79   "Jumping Exercises", *Athletic Coach* (Gt. Britain), September, pp. 8-10.

80   "A Pillar of Strength", *Track and Field Journal* (Canada), no. 11, October, p. 16.

81   "Sprint and Hurdle Skill Development", *Track and Field Journal* (Canada), no. 11, October, p. 24, 32.

82   "The Autogenic Way", *Track and Field Journal* (Canada), no. 11, October, p. 31.

83   "Cable Exercises", *OTFA Technical Bulletin* (Canada), Summer, pp. 1-2.

84   "Special Starting Exercises", *Track Technique Annual* 1981 (USA), Fall. Reprinted in *OTFA Technical Bulletin* (Canada), no. 36, Fall, pp. 10-12.

1982

85   "Kratochvilova – Athletics Begin at 30", *Modern Athlete and Coach* (Australia), April, pp. 7-9. Reprinted with similar title in *Ontario Athletics* (Canada), June, pp. 7-9. A very similar article is attributed to Miroslav Kvac (Kratochvilova's coach) in *United States Track and Field Quarterly Review*, vol. 84, no. 2, Summer 1981, pp. 18-22. Kvac acknowledges the use of the tables from the *Ontario Athletics* article by McFarlane. Both McFarlane and Kvac indicate that material for the articles came from a presentation by E. Dostal at the XI European Track and Field Coaches' Congress in Venice, 1981.

86   "Tatiana Anisimova", *Ontario Athletics* (Canada), December, pp. 20-21.

87   "Jumping Exercises", *United States Track & Field Quarterly*, vol. 82, no. 4., pp. 54-55.

1983

88 "Use of Proper Energy Systems in Training, *Track Technique* (USA), no. 84, Spring, pp. 2685-2689. Reprinted as "Energy Systems Simplified" in *Modern Athlete and Coach* (Australia), vol. 21, no. 2, April, pp. 3-7 and in *OTFA Technical Bulletin* (Canada), no. 41, Winter, pp.1-8. The *OTFA Technical Bulletin* article contains one more table.

89 "Strength – A Different Dimension", *Track Technique* (USA), no. 85, Summer, pp. 2704-2705.

90 "Charlie Francis – Sprint Success in Canada", *Track and Field Journal* (Canada), no. 23, October, pp. 26-27.

1984

91 "Simplified Circuit Training", *Track Technique* (USA), no. 88 Spring, pp. 2797-2798. Reprinted in *United States Track and Field Quarterly Review*, vol. 84, no. 2, Summer, pp. 46-48.

92 "Speed Endurance – Rhythm Sequencing", *United States Track and Field Quarterly Review*, vol. 84, no. 2, Summer, p. 31.

93 "The Women's 100m Hurdles (Szczepanski)", *United States Track and Field Quarterly Review*, vol. 84, no. 2, Summer, pp. 34-37. Reprinted with minor editing changes in Modern Athlete and Coach (Australia), October 1984, pp. 15-18.

94 "Helsinki Report, 100m Hurdles", *United States Track and Field Quarterly Review*, vol. 84, no. 2, Summer, pp. 40-41. Reprinted as "Womens 100m Hurdles (Helsinki)" in *Modern Athlete and Coach* (Australia), January pp. 7-9 and as "No static stretching, eh?" in *Coaching Review* (Canada), vol. 7, no. 3, pp. 47-48. The Coaching Review article has minor changes.

95 "Special Strength – Horizontal or Vertical", *United States Track and Field Quarterly Review*, vol. 84, no. 2, Summer, pp. 51-54.

96   "Sequencing Speed – A Basic Pattern", *Track and Field Journal* (Canada), no. 25, February, pp. 28-29.

97   "Developing Maximum Running Speed", *Sports*, September, 1984. (A series of monographs published by the Coaching Association of Canada.) The article is reprinted in similar form in *National Strength and Conditioning Association Journal*, vol. 6, no. 5, October, pp. 24-28.

98   Pickering, R.J., *Strength Training for Athletes*, London: British Amateur Athletic Board, 1968.

99   Radford, P., "Scientific Bases of Sprint Performance", *Athletic Coach* (England), vol. 10, no. 2, 3, June-September, 1976.

100   Robinson, W.P., "The Achievement Motive", *British Journal of Social and Clinical Psychology*, 4, 1964, pp. 98-103.

101   Schmolinsky, G., *Track and Field*, Berlin, German Democratic Republic: Sportverlag, 1978.

102   Singer, R., *Motor Learning and Human Performance*, NY: Macmillan Co, 1968.

103   Suinn, Richard. *Seven Steps to Peak Performance: The Mental Training Manual for Athletes.* Toronto, Lewiston, Berne, Stuttgart: Hans Huber Publishers, 1986.

104   Tschiene, P., *Notes from the Third Annual OTFA Coach Seminar*, Lake Couchiching, Ontario, Canada, October, 1977.

105   Tschiene, P., "The Annual Training Schedule and General Principles", *Technical Bulletin*, 1, 1978, pp. 6-12.

106   Verhoshansky, Y., "Depth Jumping in the Training of Jumpers", *Legaya Atletika* (USSR), 1967. (Translated in *United States Track and Field Quarterly Review*, vol. 79, no. 1 Spring, 1979, p. 60.)

[107] Wilt, Fred, "From the Desk of Fred Wilt – Plyometric Exercises", *Track Technique*, no. 64, June, 1976, p. 2024.

[108] Yessis, Michael, *Proceedings of Conference 1982*, Ottawa: Canadian Track and Field Association, 1982.

Manuals and Handbooks
[109] International Amateur Athletics Federation Handbook, London: IAAF, The handbook used in the preparation of this book is the 1985/86 edition.

[110] McFarlane, B., *Level 2 (Sprints, Hurdles, Relays) Course Conductor Guide*, Ottawa: Canadian Track & Field Association, 1982.

[111] *National Coaching Certification Program: Coaching Theory, Level 3*, Ottawa: Coaching Association of Canada, 1981.

[112] *National Coaching Certification Program: Coaching Theory, Level 2*, Ottawa: Coaching Association of Canada, 1979.